Artists of the West

A collection of works by notable artists throughout the western United States

Cameron Blagg III
Dave Bartholet
Cameron Blagg
Leta Brown

Skamania Mines Publishing
For more information on "Northwest Artists," future editions or book signings
please contact Cameron Blagg III at cameroniii@aol.com,
2908 Pine Street SE, Albany, Oregon 97322 • 503.932.2324

Dedicated to Margaret and Estel Bolman

Cover Credits

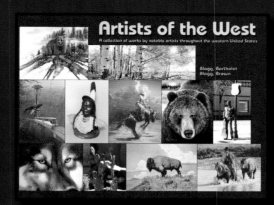

Artists featured on the front cover are:

Dave Bartholet - Spring Break

Gary Love - Break on Through

Tim Wistrom - Current Events

Cameron Blagg - Chief Joseph Bronze

Robert Krogle - On the Rise

Roby Baer - Eye to Eye

Ron Adamson - Standing on a Corner

Lee Johnson - Eyes of the Wolf

Kim and Stephen Davis - Oasis Copper Fountain

Ken Hurley - His Land

Karen Boylan - Knee Deep and Rising

Artists featured on the back cover are:

Gary Holland - The Gift

Don Shafer - Three New Boats

Chris Mooney - Burnside Bridge

Gerald Roberts - Brave Dog Dancer

Don Begg - Annie and Teddy

Molly Kubista

Bill Carnahan - Days Gone By

Diane Martinez

Rosalind Phillips - Penguin Friends

Terry Maddox - North Head Lighthouse

Marie Gunton - La Rueda

Table of Contents

Table of Contents

Table of Contents

Friends of the Artists

Fred Oldfield
Freer Fine Art Printing
ProShot Imaging
Steve Mitzner
Port of Ilwaco Sat Market
Jay Contway
FrameWorks
Izzy Fletcher
Gilbert District Gallery
Dotty Light
Denise Bruchman
Western Reflections
KC Gallery
Don Ross Art Gallery
Inspiration Glass
E-Powersellers
Gallery 12
National Fine Arts Show
Darla Reed
Ellensburg Art Show

Introduction

For many years a regular contributor to Liberty, the Saturday Evening Post, Esquire and Colliers, Bill Gulick has published sixteen novels, several of which have been turned into movies such as Bend of the River, Road to Denver and Hallelujah Trail. His first non-fiction book, Snake River Country (Caxton, 1971), which is now in its 4th printing, was given the Pacific Northwest Booksellers Award as the Best Non-Fiction Book of the Year.

He has written and produced three Historical Outdoors Dramas, most recently Trails West, which dealt with events occurring from the time of the Lewis and Clark Expedition in 1805 through the signing of the Stevens Treaties in 1855. This production was selected by the United States Department of Commerce as one of America's Top Ten Family Spectaculars for 1976.

Making his home in Walla Walla for the past thirty years, he has worked with the Nez Perces, Umatillas, Walla Wallas, Cayuses, and Yakamas on a number of projects whose purpose has been to bring about a better understanding of Indian land, water, fishing, and sovereignty rights. In 1976, he was Project Director for a $24,000 Washington State Humanities Commission Grants given Trails West, in conjunction with Whitman College and the Whitman Mission National Historic Site, to pay Indian advisors and actors performing in the production and to hold eleven public forums in which Indian and white experts discussed Indian Treaty rights.

Bill is past President of Western Writers of America, Inc. Two of his Saturday Evening Post stories have won the organization's prestigious Spur Award as Best Western Short Story of the Year.

-This excerpt taken from Chief Joseph Country - Land of the Nez Perce by Bill Gulick

My interest in Western Art began while I was writing stories for magazines such as the Saturday Evening Post, Liberty, and Colliers. Before publication, my story would be given to an artist who would illustrate it with a painting of a western scene. When I later wrote the Art Director and told him I liked the painting, he would pass my letter on to the artist, who often would give me the original—for which he had been well paid—in hopes that I would suggest that he be chosen to illustrate the next story I sold to that particular magazine. In this manner, I began to fill my study walls with paintings done by artists such as Edwin Marsh, Paul Rabut, Al Schmidt, Fred Ludekens, Carl Grohe and others.

When I wrote my non-fiction book, Chief Joseph Country, Dave Manuel, an artist friend in Walla Walla, did the painting used as a book jacket. After selling the original for a good price, he gave me the remarqued "Artist's Proof," then asked me if I would serve as "Honorary Chairman" of the Ellensburg, Washington, Western Art Show in late May, 1979.

"What does an Honorary Chairman do?" I asked.

"Nothing much. He just meets the artists and says nice things about their paintings, then makes a speech before the Saturday night auction."

"What should I talk about?"

Dave was silent for a moment, then smiled and said, "Why don't you talk about five minutes, then sit down and let the artists sell their paintings?"

During the three days the show lasted, I met the ninety artists who were there, admired their works, and had no difficulty finding nice things to say about them. One of the first artists I met was Cameron Blagg, who a few years earlier had begun his professional career. When one of his paintings was shown during the auction, I bought it and added it to my growing collection. During the next twenty years, I attended Western Art Shows in Ellensburg and Spokane, Washington; Great Falls, Montana; Portland, Eugene, and Klamath Falls, Oregon, as well as viewing Western Art galleries in Oklahoma, Texas, and New Mexico. Along the way, I wrote a dozen articles about Western Art and Artists for magazines and acquired 35 or so paintings, bronzes, and prints by artists whose works I admired such as John Clymer, Barbara Peets, Robert Monroe, Don Crook, Fred Oldfield, Norman Adams, and others.

In every case, my reason for buying a piece of art was that it told a story about the West that intrigued me. For example, the Cameron Blagg painting was a portrait of an old Indian in a desert setting, the deep wrinkles etched in his weathered face resembling the fissures in the Grand Canyon itself, denoting the thousands of years his ancestors had lived in that part of the country and the millions of years of erosion it had taken to carve out the Canyon. Since that time, other paintings, murals, and bronzes done by Cameron Blagg have told similar stories just as well.

So my standards are clear: I like a piece of art that tells a story. Included in the first collection published by Cameron Blagg III, Northwest Artists, were many pieces that did that. I'm sure that those in this collection will do the same, for the talent of its artists is just as high.

---Bill Gulick

Recognition and Appreciation

ay Coates
466 West Jump Off Joe Road
alley, Washington 99181
lcircl@theofficenet.com

m Reed
O Box 426
yrtle Creek, Oregon 97457
antheotlr@yahoo.com

aul Howard
504 Cottonwood Drive
chland, Washington 99354
oward3bpc@aol.com
09)539-gold

In recognition of RJ Lee Group, Inc.'s extending their collective hand in goodwill in both respect and technology, The Great Sioux Nation of Lakota, Dakota, and Nakota, presented this gift of collective artists' contributions. This symbol was presented to the laboratory director at the Center for Laboratory Sciences on the campus of Columbia Basin College, Pasco, Washington.

Marlene Locke, full-blood Lakota, descended from Treaty Chief Blunt Horn (Short Horn), offers this gesture of recognition as Delegate of the L.D.N. people in joint approval with Grand Chief Richard Grass, descendant of Chief Charging Bear, Chief Sitting Bull, Chief Red Cloud, Chief Two Strike, Chief White Swan, Chief White Bird, and Old

Chief Frost. Both are aware of and respect RJ Lee Group, Inc.'s assistance and contribution to the community here, including The Confederated Tribes of the Umatilla, and The Nez Perce.

Symbolism — The foundation or red rock signifies the Badlands, sacred ground to The Sioux Nation People. Supported by the earth, the deer antler extends with life and traditional sustenance. The blade, made from roller chain, and forged in fire by Jay Coates, a fire keeper and Farrier, was pounded like a drum with his hammer as a stick, and with a prayer in his heart that the Red and White Nations or First and Second Nations will once again work together respectfully. The Blood wood handle secured with rawhide has typically been used by Mr. Coates for high recognition pieces that have gone to cultural, spiritual, and traditional leaders from North Carolina to the Pacific Coast. Encouraged in his early years by Cameron Blagg, Coates continues to "forge ahead" with respect. The circle of life, done in ivory, contributed by coastal Native Americans and crafted by Paul Howard, frames and protects the cross Cannupas, or "sacred peace pipes." This

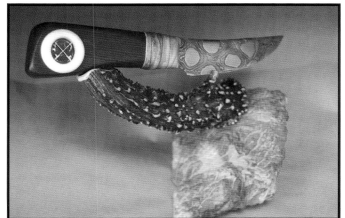

first authorized use by the L.D.N. Chiefs Association and cognizant of the Sioux legend symbolizing First and Second Nation People working together again, was also done by Howard in 18-karat gold and 10% iridium platinum. The background was done by Tim Reed whose grandmother was full-blood Cherokee and has woven in the four colors of people and directions including the red(W), black(N), yellow(E), and white(S) seen typically on the Lakota symbol of the Wheel of Life. Centered in Reed's "Intarsia" art form, done all in stone, is fire opal from Ethiopia contributed by Amde Zewdalem and crafted by Reed to be symbolic not only of Mother Earth but also the fire of the heart. This symbolic work is the first collaborative piece of this small circle of artists in respect for the larger circle to which RJ Lee Group, Inc. with analytical, characterization, and educational expertise is appreciated as a contributing part of the solution.

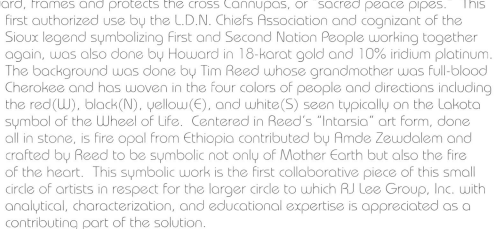

cameron blagg

Wranglin'

American Maid

Cameron and his wife, Pamela, live in a cabin that they built in the mountains on the edge of the Cabinet Range Wilderness in Northwest Montana. Much of his inspiration is derived from this natural setting where they live and work and try to do their part in keeping many of the old ways alive.

Moon Lit Meadow

Thunder Rolling Over The Mountains

Huckleberry Time

Professional Artist Since 1974

PO Box 91
Noxon, Montana 59853
(406) 295-9650

PO Box 881
Albany, Oregon 97321
(503) 932-2324

Artist E-mail: LatteCoyote@frontiernet.net
Cameron Blagg III E-mail: cameroniii@aol.com

Website: www.cameronblagg.com

Tim Wistrom

Smooth Sailing

Time Flies

Seattle Harbour

Renowned professional artist, Tim Wistrom has established himself as an innovative and unique modern master of realism and surrealism. His realistic scenes are marine and nature images, while the surrealistic paintings ponder a "what if?" view of the future. The basic premise behind his surrealism is nature comes back and reclaims the world, which continues to go through geological changes.

Tim works with Acrylic on Canvas, and has produced countless Original Paintings as well as Limited Edition Prints and Giclees (archival prints on canvas). His works are widely collected for their thought provoking themes and attention to detail. His prints are in high demand because he usually limits his editions to 950; his images wildly go up in value on the secondary market.

Born in Germany to parents in the US Air Force, Tim grew up in Germany, on the East Coast, in San Diego, and Seattle. Although his travels take him all over the world, Washington has been his home for almost 25 years.

Extreme

Current Events

Lost Vegas

Liberty Awake

A Class Act Gallery
www.timwistrom.com

POB 797 / 612 S. 1st Street
La Conner, WA 98257
360-466-2000

Tim painted this in response to the 9/11 attacks. The Twin Towers are gone, but the reflection of them indicates that we will never forget that day. And the Statue, our symbol of Liberty & Freedom, has come off her pedestal to go over to help

Natural Passage

Penney Lockhart of Tombiglee Studio

If you like detail, you will want a Lockhart

Welcome to Tombiglee Studio

A gift from God is her talent to create her art. All Penney Lockhart ever wanted to be was a Fine Artist. No other profession seemed to interest her more then this. Her mediums are watercolor, ink and sand. As of late she is working on honoring her grandmother's memory by acquiring her grandmothers name, "White Fawn." Her favorite subjects are Native American, but she also portrays wildlife and western subjects. Sands are previewed on this page including the background of "The Painted Hills of John Day Fossil Beds." Craft sand, glass sand and natural sands are used in these pieces. She will blend the skin color to match the person. Highlighting the lines in the faces with watercolor to make them stand out and give you the illusion of a three dimensional view. Her texture of the fur or bead work jump out at you. No mole or dimple is left out. The eyes of her faces will watch you, the shadow from the nose is from the nose. They are truly one of kind. She has her sand pieces in the Pendleton Roundup and Happy Canyon Hall of Fame, Pendleton, Oregon and the Appaloosa Museum, in Moscow, Idaho.

Lately she has had fun doing illustrations for children's story books. She has found its fun to see a story come to life for a child's eyes. She gets into designing cards too with a comical bent, for Holidays or everyday.

So, check her out at www.penneylockhart.com or write her or call if you have any questions. Her address is PO Box 213 Burley, Washington 98322-0213 / phone 360.895.1707 / fax 360.874.8546.

Princess Angeline, Dwamish

Saquamish Blessing

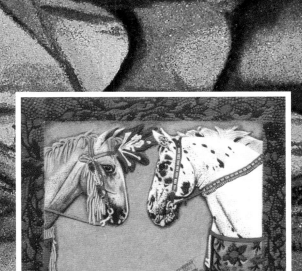

Head to Head

The Imagination of Tombiglee Studio

*magination...
I was called a dreamer
by my teachers
in Elementary School*

A true artist thrives on
their imagination.

I probably was...

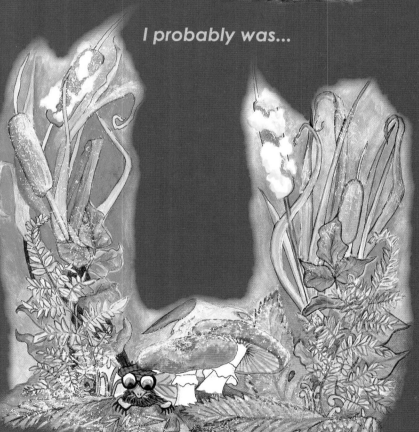

And if they are
kept from it they
will wither away.

But look what this
imagination did for
a dreamer, along
with a great story.

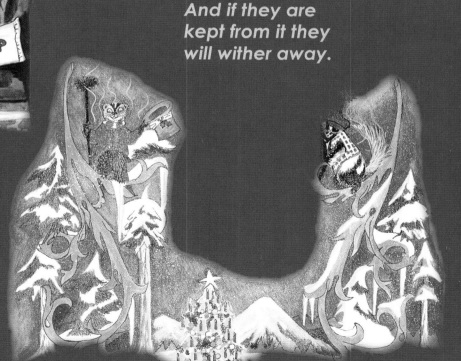

Don and Shirley Begg

Don has been an international award winning professional sculptor for 38 years. Born and raised on a cattle ranch, he has been a keen observer of wildlife from the Rocky Mountains to Africa and the outback of Australia.

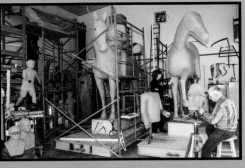

Having completed courses in sculpture and art casting, Don interned in the California studio of noted monumental bronze sculptor Franco Vianello followed by intensive study of monumental sculpture at Hoheb Studios in New York.

Shirley Begg B.Sc. Chemistry is a 2nd generation bronze sculptor and the daughter of famous illustrator and Western sculptor, Doug Stephens.

Since 1970 Don and Shirley have owned and operated the fine art foundry Studio West Ltd. providing complete sculpture services, miniature to monumental design, enlargements, mold making, lostwax bronze casting, patina, plinthe design and installation. They are personally involved in each stage of the casting and finishing of each bronze sculpture and statue.

The Begg's limited edition bronzes appear in international private, corporate and museum art collections on 5 continents including the collection of Her Majesty Queen Elizabeth II.

Don and Shirley Begg's Studio West Ltd. is located at 205-2 Ave SE Box 550 Cochrane, Alberta Canada T4C 1A7.

"Don Begg is now recognized internationally as a master of monumental scale sculpture...Mr. Begg has clearly won the approval of the people and institutions responsible for Canada's public art" [excerpt from the Alberta Achievement Awards Presentation].

Well known for highly detailed and historically accurate lifelike monumental bronzes, Don and Shirley have completed more than 100 bronze statues for public buildings, schools, libraries, airports, museums, parks, cenotaphs, military monuments and residential communities across North America and in Europe.

Life-size limited edition bronzes currently available: children at play, blackbear, cougar, flyfisherman, duck hunter, rodeo bull rider, rock climber, jumping white tail deer, trout, children reading, a pioneer woman feeding chickens, a young soccer player and Canadian geese.

Annie and Teddy

Jumping Whitetail Buck

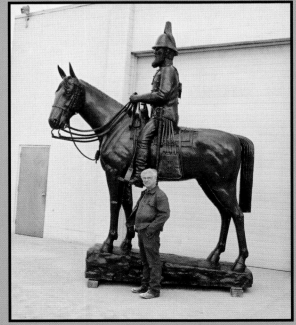

Colonel James Macleod and Don Begg

Major General William Griesbach

Building The Grade

Cowsense

Marsh Beauties

BEGGS

Patina and Ross

Gary Kerby

"He Came From The Dark Timber"

P.O. Box 391
Wilsall, Montana 59086

www.garykerbyart.com

Gary was born into a third generation ranching family near Toppenish, Washington and began painting at an early age. While taking painting lessons from noted Western artist Don Crook in 1981, Gary began to realize his potential. With Don's mentoring and encouragement, Gary made art a career choice.

With the love of the west in his blood, Gary created work with an emphasis on old west culture during much of his early career. Working with his hometown community, Gary painted a collector series of 10 rodeo posters celebrating the area's ranching heritage. For nine years, Gary traveled the west and Midwest, designing and painting 43 murals for towns in California, Washington, Oregon, Montana and Illinois. In 1995, Gary proudly created a bronze sculpture of 5-time world bareback

bronc champion, Bruce Ford, which went on permanent display in the Pro Rodeo hall of Fame in Colorado Springs, Colorado.

In 1998, change was in the air, and Gary moved to the big sky country of Montana. "First and foremost I have always been an outdoors man," says Kerby. "Secondly, I'm an artist. With my love of wild country and adventure it only seemed natural for me to be painting landscapes and animals – and what better place than the wilds of south central Montana". Gary relocated 80 miles north of Yellowstone National Park, near Livingston, Montana. "Natural beauty surrounds my home," says Kerby, "not a day goes by that I don't find inspiration in a deer wandering through my yard, the sound of a sandhill crane at dawn or the evening sun on the Crazy Mountains."

The abundant new inspiration Gary enjoys translated to numerous one-man shows and commissioned works. Most recently, Kerby was commissioned to create a life-size bronze mountain man for the community of Wilsall, Montana. This work, a gateway sculpture celebrates the Shields Valley area's discovery and heritage. In 2007, Gary was asked to create the 75th anniversary rodeo poster for Toppenish, Washington and was named Lead Artist for that community's "Mural in a Day" art project.

Kerby invites us into his creative experience, "My hope is, all of you will travel with me to the wild places, experience wild creatures and feel what I felt though the work I create. Take a walk with me. Let's see where the journey takes us."

"Wild Montana Skies"

Gary's Lifesize Bronze - "Welcome to the Shields"

"An Evening At Rifle Falls"

"Two of a Kind"

9447 Gant Road
Bozeman, Montana 59718
406.586.1564
www.kboylanart.com

The Fine Art of

Karen Boylan

I can only describe my art as a passion! From an early age I was always fascinated by animals and nature; contrast in colors, movement, the effect of light on objects, and the infinite detail of everything from grasses, rocks, and leaves to the majestic mountains in which I live.

Still ranching after 34 years, I can draw from my experience to create the detailed paintings people have come to recognize. Attention to detail is the most important aspect of my work - I strive for accuracy and realism in every piece. Although I work in acrylic, gouache, pencil, and scratch board, the last few years have been devoted mainly to oil. Hopefully, with each new painting, my passion will push me to new heights and help me to grow as an artist.

"Cautious Crossing"

"Restless"

"Knee Deep & Rising"

"Chelsea"

"Soaking Wet"

Member of
The
Western Art
Association,
Western
Heritage
Artists
and
Northwest
Artists.

"Crossing the Cheyenne"

Karen Boylan

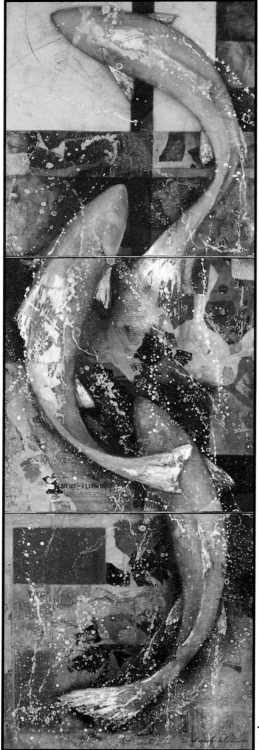

Jennifer Williams

Born and raised in the Pacific Northwest, the power of nature is my greatest influence. I have devoted my work to the exploration of environmental issues inspired by the contrasts that occur when nature is viewed as society's resource. Whether it is the unnatural patterns created by managed forests, or the strategic re-routing of a stream, these scenes have become a part of our landscape.

Living in a community that rests upon the shores of the Columbia River, we are dependant upon many of the natural resources the Pacific Northwest provides. The condition of wild salmon has come to symbolize the vulnerability of the natural ecosystem. In my series entitled "Endangered Ritual," I strive to show the strength and perseverance of nature, while questioning the imbalance caused by our own presence.

My medium is paper collage and acrylic on wood. Thick layering of recycled fragmented paper and translucent paint provides a lush base. Meticulous scratching and sanding creates a raw surface that becomes an integral part of the painting as bits and pieces of the text, maps, and images are revealed. I work each composition stimulated by fragmented abstraction with little pre-conception. As a result, each piece is a new discovery. I paint anticipating that moment when the painting takes on a life of its own.

▲ Watershed
48" x 48"

▲ Counting Salmon
48" x 48"

▲ Coming Home
48" x 48"

◀ Tier
24" x 72"

www.jenniferwilliamsfineart.com

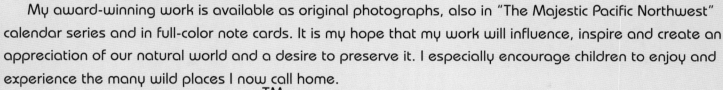

Nancy J. Smith
Nature Photographer

www.nancyjsmith.biz

Since 1990, I have been exploring the beauty of the Pacific Northwest and sharing it through my photography. Nature is a gift to treasure and showcasing it in its purest state is my passion. All full-color images are shot under natural light, on film, without the use of colored filters or digital manipulation.

My award-winning work is available as original photographs, also in "The Majestic Pacific Northwest" calendar series and in full-color note cards. It is my hope that my work will influence, inspire and create an appreciation of our natural world and a desire to preserve it. I especially encourage children to enjoy and experience the many wild places I now call home.

"Remember to Appreciate Nature"™

Oregon Coast Sunset

Last Light on the Mountain

Multnomah Falls

Oregon Grape

Puzzle Creek

Pelican at Sea

Bart Miller

Born in Portland, Oregon in 1959, Bart has a deep inner passion for the outdoors, wrought from his lifetime of experiences, which began as a youngster following along behind grandpa to the fishing hole for a day of cherished memories. He enjoys time in the outdoors as much now as he did when he was growing up in the small community of Scappoose, Oregon. He treasures the time he spends with his family, Raquel "Rocky" Miller, wife and greatest aficionado and with his three children and grandchildren. Employed full-time at a local credit union, Bart still finds time to remain active in his community by volunteering for several functions and organizations.

A lifetime of outdoor excursions; camping, hunting and fishing in the Oregon territory from the high lakes to the Oregon Coast along with his passion for the past and natural history is the motivation behind his work which is revealed in his renderings.

Bart, a self-taught and naturally gifted artist first discovered his talent while attempting to amuse his son by drawing cartoon characters. Surprised at the outcome and the ease with which it flowed, he sought counsel and support to learn more about how to cultivate his new-found gift. As providence would have it, he had the good fortune to chance upon world-renowned wildlife artist Dave Bartholet, who affirmed his talent and mentored his abilities; building confidence and belief in the gift he had been given.

Bart uses a variety of mixed media but prefers graphite, watercolor, and pastels. His specialty lies in graphite pencil drawings where optimal detail is articulated and brought to what appears to be a realistic and life-like image.

He has participated in a number of local cultural events where his art work has been on display. You may also find his collection on exhibit at the Lofted Lair Gallery located in St. Helens, Oregon, The Gilbert District Gallery in Seaside, Oregon, as well as various locations in Astoria, Oregon and Ilwaco, Washington where he hopes to spend his retirement years.

Bart is a member of the National Independent Artist Association and The North Coast Creative Artist Association. He was also the featured artist during the March 2007 Clatskanie Cultural Coalition event.

"It is my sincere wish and greatest hope that these works of art will bring you as much joy when you view them as I experienced while creating them"

Shipwreck

Chickadee

The Charge

Lofted Lair Gallery
290 South First Street
St. Helens, Oregon 97051

www.artbybart.net

503.543.2202

artbybartmiller@gmail.com

The Lighthouse

Setting Sail

Bart Miller 27

ALEXANDRA SCHILLER

EINSTEIN'S OBSERVATION THAT "THE MONOTONY OF A QUIET LIFE STIMULATES THE MIND" MIGHT EXPLAIN MY COMPULSION TO DRAW AND PAINT! AN ACTIVE IMAGINATION NEEDS LITTLE TO INSPIRE IT, ALTHOUGH I AM ESPECIALLY MOTIVATED BY EXAMPLES OF THE POWER OF THE CREATIVE SPIRIT; E.G.: NATURE'S AWESOME ENERGY AND MAN'S UNIQUE ARCHITECTURAL DESIGNS.

MY WORK - OIL ON STRETCHED CANVAS AND A FEW WATER COLORED SKETCHES - HAS BEEN SHOWN THROUGHOUT THE WESTERN UNITED STATES FROM BOISE, IDAHO TO SAN DIEGO, CALIFORNIA.

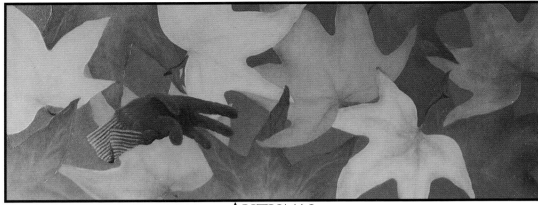

AUTUMN

COQUILLE, OREGON
541.396.3737

CORDOBA

THE MARKETPLACE

DJERBA

Jo Dunnick

mail: jodunnick@rio.com
Website: www.jodunnick.com
Phone: 541.937.3641

82295 Rattlesnake Road • Dexter, Oregon 97431

Jo Dunnick, while a relative newcomer to the world of watercolor art, has for many years been an artist in other mediums. Her art has been showcased in stained glass, calligraphy, leather and jewelry. In 2000, drawn to the lightness and flow of watercolor, Jo began her journey as a watercolorist. Her pieces include Native American, western, animal and landscape themes. While some paintings are painstakingly planned and controlled, "others," Jo muses, "seem to paint themselves." Using a technique of doing the background first and then allowing the paper and paint to dictate the subject has resulted in some of her most captivating work.

In Jo's words: "I've been told that my paintings have a lot of motion, moving some people to tears...or laughter. I appreciate that someone can be touched by the colors I have used and the subjects that have chosen to appear. Sometimes it feels that way...that there are animals or people who have been waiting to show themselves and choose to do so on my paper. However it happens is fine with me. I love the process and celebrate the outcome. I hope that my watercolors catch your eye and capture your heart."

"Ceremonial Spirit Dancer"

"Trail's End"

"In The Morning"

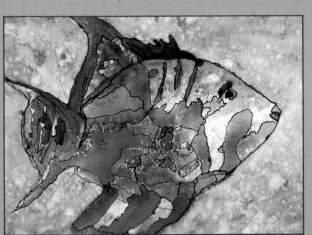

"Reed's Fish"

"Hannah's Bear"

"In The Presence of Greatness"

Sue Boswell

At the age of five years, Sue Boswell's artwork was entered in the County Fair at Pomona, California. Since these early days, her life has been clearly marked with a passion for creative expression. For her, art is a form of praising God … an appreciation for His creation. "When I paint, I actually transcend into what I am painting," Sue explains. "I become a part of the tree or the cloud that I am painting and it becomes God's expression through me."

Living in Jackson, Wyoming for 7 years gave Sue the opportunity to convey nature in a new light. Mountains and oceans are among her favorite subjects although watercolor is her preferred medium. Using an extensive amount of pigment to bring out extreme color depth is her trademark. The end result is a watercolor with so much detail that many believe it to be an oil painting. Her technique combines realism and impressionism creating an almost mystical experience. You are invited to enjoy the "gentle" world expressed through the unique art of Sue Boswell.

Sawtooth Panorama

Sammie Ben and Nikki

Olivia

www.imagemaker.org/artist/sueboswell

Lighthouse Solitude

Above It All

Mt. McGown Reflections

KARA KRIEGER-MCGHEE

Custom Murals & Fine Art

Kara is native to the Northwest and new to the art world,
although she has drawn and painted all her life. She is a self-taught
artist who enjoys painting wildlife, particularly birds,
experimenting with landscapes and portraits and painting murals.
You can learn more about the artist on her website.

www.karamcghee.com

email: kara@karamcghee.com

360.921.0870

Strutting His Stuff

Reflections

Riding The Goat Cart

Polly

Bozeman Ruins

Brad Quist

www.quistartstudio.com

Raised in Montana, Brad spent his childhood experiencing a wide variety of mountain, lake and river scenery during family camping and fishing trips. He developed a respect and passion for the outdoors and wildlife that established the inspiration for his art today. It wasn't long until this outdoor appreciation manifested itself into a desire to draw and paint. "I was one of those kids that was always drawing or creating something."

When he moved to Oregon in 1991 his goal was to work with youth, something that he had done since he graduated from high school. "I was interested in helping kids and involving myself in building up our young people by either coaching, teaching or mentoring." After working for the YMCA and Boys Club in Montana he spent twelve years in Portland, Oregon working for the Juvenile Justice System. "During this time I continued to reflect on my true passion - blending my love for the outdoors with my creativity." This inspired Brad to develop a visual art program to teach at risk youth the elements of art.

In 1998 Brad became more serious about his aspiration in the art world. He started entering his work into small local shows, national fish stamp competitions and national conservation stamp competitions which include: Wyoming's Conservation Stamp, Pennsylvania's Trout Stamp and Delaware's Trout Stamp. "I always knew that a fishing theme was close to my heart so I totally became a student and immersed myself into painting rivers, lakes and fishing scenes. I wasn't sure where this was going to lead, but I knew that I couldn't stop thinking about painting and creating compositions."

Brad is now fully immersed into his art and participates in a variety of art festivals, sportsman shows and fishing events every year in the Northwest. Having won a few awards along the way he feels he is established as a professional artist. Brad and his family currently live in the Willamette Valley where he is a full-time artist and dad. "It's great being home with my kids and doing what I love. I'm very thankful I am able to have a job where I am free to create."

Dancing Browns

Oregon Browns

Fishing Hole

Fall Steelies

ROBY BAER PSA

WWW.ROBYS.COM

Roberta "Roby" Baer is a Signature Member of the Pastel Society Of America. She is a self-taught artist specializing in the medium of pastels and was inspired by both her Mother and Grandmother, watching them paint with pastels and oils en plein air in her formative years. Her attention to detail was also inspired by Norman Rockwell, Robert Bateman and Carl Brenders. Roby's early love of nature, encouraged by parents who loved fishing and hiking in wilderness areas, has given her a vast knowledge of both animals and their habitat, helping to achieve photo realism in her images.

She is internationally recognized and has been published in the "International Artist Magazine," (Master Painter Showcase), as well as "finalist" position in "The Artist Magazine" annual art competition. Roby has been chosen winner of the City of Redding call to artists for a rendition of the world famous architect Santiago Calatrava's "Sundial Bridge" in Redding, California and Artist of The Year for the Dove Sportsman's Society 2005/06 with stamp. Roby was "Artist of the Year" 2003/04 for Quail Unlimited with three covers on their magazine; honors of celebrating three "firsts" in the 22-year old conservation stamp/print program: the first pastel medium, the first female artist and the first vertical stamp image. She has been awarded "Best in Show" and juried art competition awards, and is represented by numerous galleries. In the spring of 2007, Roby also received recognition in the Pastel Journal Magazine in the Pastel Pointers section for "Call of The Wild."

PHAT CAT"   12 x 16 PASTEL

FLY FISHING"   12 x 16 PASTEL

"ROCKAWAY BEACH"   8 x 10 PASTEL

"MANE ATTRACTION"   11 x 14 PASTEL

PETER X O'BRIEN
watercolors

Artist, Peter X O'Brien was born in Glen Cove, New York. His family moved to Wellesley, Massachusetts and then to San Francisco, California before finally settling down in Lake Oswego, Oregon. His interest in art was encouraged at an early age by his artistic mother. Peter has been drawing and painting ever since.

Peter earned a football scholarship to the University of Idaho. He spent 4 years in Idaho playing collegiate football and studying drawing and painting. In 1985, Pete signed as a placekicker with the New Orleans Saints. After a brief career in the NFL, He decided to go back to school and complete his college education. He graduated with a BA in Fine Arts from the University of Oregon.

Pete lives in West Linn, Oregon with his wife and children and has a studio in Lake Oswego. He still finds time to travel extensively looking for fresh subject matter to paint. He has studied under well known artists such as Tom Lynch, Tony Couch, Jan Kunz, Jim Ponti and Eric Wiegardt in his persistent quest to expand and refine his craft.

Pete is considered by his peers as one of the emerging western artists and is participating in juried art shows throughout the west. He was awarded 3 "Best of Show" honors in 2005.

"Long, Tall Drink O' Water"

"Tumalo Landscape"

"Get Along Duke"

Peter X O'Brien
1547 11th Street
West Linn, Oregon 97068

(503) 655-9373

www.peterobrienwatercolors.com

"Puerto Penasco Shrimp Boats"

"Early Watering"

Great Egret 2 - 11 x 15

Wendy Thompson, CPSA
Colored Pencil Society of America – Signature Member
www.wthompsonart.com

I was born and raised in Oregon; the Pacific Northwest offers a continually changing palette from which to draw inspiration. My studio shelves are filled with reference books and collections of bugs, feathers and dragonflies that I refer to for the accuracy and detail recognized in my work. I work with subjects of Nature rendered in colored pencil, brought to life with a flare of whimsy.

A lot of time and patience is required to complete a colored pencil painting, and inexorably it is this same quiet time that fills specific therapeutic and meditative needs in my life. When I am working, my thoughts return to the quiet places of the woods and ponds, and I strive to emulate this in my work. If you feel a sense of quietude and tranquility when viewing my paintings, then I have been successful in conveying my thoughts and feelings to you through my work, and have hopefully given you a quiet place of your own.

Great Egret 1 - 11 x 15

Blue Window - 10.5 x 8.25

Winter Raven - 10 x 10

Spring Raven - 10 x 10

Solomon Seal - 7 x 7

Days Lost & Little - 12 x 8.5

The Ladies - 9 x 13

Lorraine Pascuzzi

Specializing in Western Art
Oil - Watercolor - Charcoal/Pencil

North Plains, Oregon

www.westernartspirit.com

Native Oregonian Lorraine Pascuzzi developed an interest in western art as a child. Her imaginative interpretation in bright colors and contemporary styles are derived from her own photography of rodeo cowboys, ranch life and regional Pow Wows. Lorraine is versatile in watercolor, pencil, oil, acrylic and pastel. She now resides with her family in the beautiful countryside of Oregon.

Shaman - 30 x 40 - oil

Eaglespeaker - 18 x 24 - oil

Sundance - 22 x 30 - watercolor

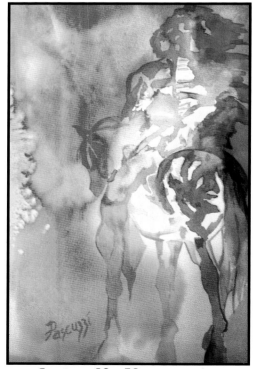

Sunrise - 22 x 30 - watercolor

Spirits of Celilo Falls - 40 x 46 - oil

Custer's Last Stand - 24 x 36 - oil

Spirit - 12 x 12 - charcoal/pencil

Summer Camp - 20 x 28 - watercolor

LeRoy Jesfield

Photo by Wanda Jesfield

LeRoy Jesfield completed his first painting, a Coyote, in Billings, Montana, when he was eight years of age. Fifty years later, wildlife and nature are both still a big slice of his life. He also enjoys painting portraits and commissioned illustrations. Acrylic on canvas or board is the artist's primary medium. Many of his paintings have hidden messages, which are intriguing to the viewer.

For more information on this artist
or to purchase artwork or prints,
please go to www.jesfieldproductions.com
or call Jesfield Studio at (360) 275-6776.
P.O. Box 1960, Belfair, Washington 98528

"Kenya Leopard"

"As a Man Soweth"

"Dawn of Creation"

"Blue Heron"

"Kenneth Hurley"

"View From Hurricane Ridge"

"Fox View" - Ollie, Montana

Angie Cook

Grandpa and Me   Graphite Pencil, 11 x 14

www.equinepencilart.com

Angie Cook is a native Northwesterner. Raised in the rural towns of North Plains and St. Helens, she has lived her whole life in Oregon where she has long enjoyed the region's four distinct seasons and tremendous natural beauty. She relishes the luxury of exploring the dessert, the beach, the mountains, and the plains at the state's four corners.

Angie's enthusiasm for Oregon and the Northwest is matched only by her passion for horses. Her love affair dates back to childhood when her mother caught her utilizing crayons to decorate her bedroom walls with images of the majestic creatures.

Angie began riding horses at seven years of age. The passion ignited, she went on to work at a horse farm when she was only fourteen. She saved her earnings to find and purchase "Topo's New Dawn," her beloved first horse. "Dawn" is a Quarter Horse mare that has now retired from numerous shows and events. Over the years, Angie participated in everything from High School Rodeo and Western Pleasure to Team Penning and Breakaway Roping.

A self-taught artist, Angie has honed her artistic skills to express her love of horses. With no formal art training beyond high school, Angie has keenly crafted an exacting and elegant signature look for her art. A wide range of equestrian work has afforded her the opportunity to study these gracious animals—to get to know their distinct personalities and the intricacies of their body build and bone structure.

Angie and her husband currently live in St. Helens where they're raising their two young children. They share their home with three Boston Terriers and two Cats.

Angie specializes in graphite and colored pencil work. She is often hired for commissioned portraits—clients include All Around Awards for local horse shows—but she also does renderings of pets upon request. Her Original Artwork along with her Prints are available for purchasing upon request or on her website.

The Bugle   Graphite Pencil, 14 x 11

The First Embrace   Graphite Pencil, 11 x 14

Equine Art

503.369.4567

equineart@comcast.net

Proud   Watercolor Pencils, 8 x 10

As a child I was inspired by both my father and my grandmother. Each enjoyed and shared with me their own original styles of photography and taught me to appreciate the simplicity

nd beauty of the world around me. As a ird generation west coast photographer, I ave made Portland, Oregon my home.

My passion for art, photography nd travel stimulates me in creating innova- e imagery. I enjoy capturing the art and egance of the world around me, wher- er that may be.

My images are captured on 35mm des. To an assortment of these I apply gital augmentation. In the digital dark- om, combining my skill as a photographer nd a digital artist, I am able to produce hat was captured in my mind's eye. My t is not so much about the tools used to ake it, but rather the interaction of color, omposition, and rhythm, in the support of e subject matter, and the feelings trans- ted through the work itself.

For me "Image Is Everything" and my iss is creating fine art photography with egance and diversity.

MARIE GUNTON
image is everything

20800 NW Rock Creek Blvd.
Portland, Oregon 97229
503.690.0228

Website:
www.mariegunton.com
Email:
marie.gunton@verizon.net

Everett Russell

Western and Wildlife Art

Every new painting is started with the same firm belief according to Everett Russell. "This is going to be the best painting I've ever done." There are many elements that go into a successful painting. Concept, composition, key, mood, color, values and perspective are a few. One element that is not stressed nearly enough is the feeling or, if one likes, the passion an artist brings to the canvas. If an artist is not emotionally involved in the painting why should the viewer become involved? Every painting, if done honestly and with feeling, is as much about the artist as it is about the subject. Life is such a race for so many people that they never stop to look at the beauty that surrounds us all. With landscapes ranging from the deserts and canyons of the southwest to the mountains and valleys of the northwest and nostalgic scenes of the old west, this artist shows that beauty. Everett has received numerous awards for his art and has had work included in the Top 100 in the Arts for the Parks Show and the Oil Painters of America Western Regional Show. He can be contacted at (509) 775-2381 or through Shadow Mountain Gallery, Jackson, Wyoming.

Out of the Sunset

Early Snow

A Bend on the San Poil

A Cold Start

GO WITH THE FLOW

"LeAnne" - 3' x 5'

"Maple Sugar" - 3' x 5'

"Aspen Meadows" - 4' x 6'

Visit our studio by appointment
in Eugene, Oregon
Call us at 541.302.6140
or email us at davissi@comcast.net

Copper Water Features

"Water Candles" - 4' x 5'

"Fernella" - 2' x 3'

Artists' Kim and Stephen Davis with their son Jake

Photo By Brian Lanker

DON BROWN

"What inspires me to paint is when elements like light, color, shape, value and texture all come together to make an otherwise ordinary scene extraordinary."

Born in Idaho Falls, Don's family relocated several times; first to New Mexico and then to Washington while he was still very young, giving him an opportunity to experience first hand the very diverse environments and cultures of the Northwest and Southwest.

As a young adult he spent time painting on the central California coast and then working on a cattle ranch in New Mexico. He currently resides in Washington State.

Although his formal training is in Illustration Art his true calling has always been Fine Art, as evidenced by the many invitations to show and awards received for his work. Most significant to Don among these are having been selected to show at the Oil Painters of America, invited to participate as a Quick Draw artist at three separate C.M. Russell Auctions, and receiving the "Best of Show" ['98] and the "John Clymer Award" ['01] at the National Western Art Show. (For a complete list of awards and shows regularly attended visit Don's website at the address above.)

"Goat Rocks From Pacific Crest Trail"

"Cave B Vineyard"

"Daily Chores"

"A Cow Boss's Time Off"

"The Night Shift"

www.donbrownart.com

dl_brown@charter.net

509.582.6993

"Soaking Up The Sun"

"No Fight Today"

"As Spring Nears"

"Everyone can appreciate the beauty of a sunset; what I strive for in my work is to share the beauty of 'everyday things', and hopefully to inspire others to recognize that beauty for themselves."

"Watch full Eyes"

"This Doc Makes House calls"

"Fruit and Flowers"

The romance of the western way of life is captured in the detailed works of artist Kaye York. Her love of horses started her drawing them at an early age, but her married life took her to the ranches of West-Central Idaho, where she lived the western life first hand.

She has captured many awards at shows throughout the Northwest. Her primary medium is acrylic but she also works with oil and pencil. Kaye tries to push the limits of her abilities to paint more with less.

Her works are available at her galley in downtown Cambridge, Idaho, open since 1991. A full line of prints, greeting cards, note pads and calendar are also available.

Heading For The Truck

Nip & Tuck

Lazy Summer Day

**Kaye York Gallery
65 North Superior - PO Box 157
Cambridge, Idaho 83610
208-257-3277
www.kayeyork.com**

RAY WILSON

WWW.WINDSPIRITPHOTOGRAPHY.COM

POINT WILSON LIGHTHOUSE

MT. RAINIER AT BOX CANYON

GRANDFATHER CUTS LOOSE THE PONIES

Courtesy of Martha Rosenberry

Ray Wilson, award winning outdoor photographer, has been a nature lover his entire life. Ray appreciates the wonders of the world and knows that opportunity and timing are two major factors getting that "great shot." It doesn't hurt to have a little skill thrown in; in fact, it's a vital ingredient.

Ray's passion for photography helps him appreciate the challenges of catching an animal off guard in its natural habitat or capturing the sun rays dancing off the petals of a blossom. His specialty in landscape scenes and wildlife (with a fondness for old buildings) has been enhanced with an abundance of opportunities in his own backyard; the great Pacific Northwest.

His travels throughout North America and Europe aren't nearly as captivating to Ray as his subjects in Alaska, as well as his homeland, Washington State. Whether it's capturing a bridge at dawn or the mood of the ocean at sunset, Ray is patient and knows nature makes the schedule.

Many have grown fond of Ray's heartfelt talent and marvel at the crispness of the sharp color he reaps from his subjects. It is refreshing to know Ray's photos are not computer enhanced.

Ray and wife Pam presently reside in the Eastern Washington community of West Richland. Ray considers this area "The Gateway" of the Pacific Northwest.

For more information on Ray's photography please visit his website at www.windspiritphotography.com or if you have questions in regard to Ray's work email him at Windspiritphoto@aol.com.

IRON CREEK FALLS

Laurie Miller

Lynnwood, Washington

www.lauriemillerart.com
email: bassnlegs@aol.com

While at Penn State studying Theatre Arts, my oil painting teacher recommended CCA (California College of Art) as a top art school to further my art studies. It was at CCA that I first played bass guitar in a band. I was working during the day in graphic design, and my resume includes designing symbol libraries, computer graphics, technical illustrations, and corporate identity, while at night I was gigging 6-7 nights a week. I painted after my gigs to unwind, in the studio between takes or during mixes. With my art, mainly the watercolor medium, I have participated in several group shows, and I have featured my art in several solo shows.

Having lived in and visited 49 out of the 50 states, I feel the West Coast states are my favorite. The strong tall evergreen trees soothe my soul. Many of my paintings feature plants and animals, which are indigenous to the Pacific Northwest. Nature is the most frequently used inspiration for my paintings.

"Its not how many times you fall down, but how many times you get back up."

Thank you for supporting my art!
Love,
Laurie Miller

Plant People

Mother Eagle

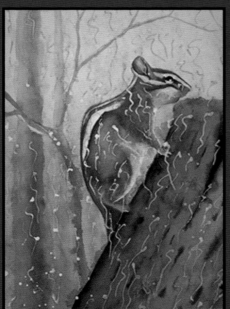

Chirpy

Our River

God's Eagles

Elk Camp

Randy McIntyre
The Natural Canvas Art Studio

Randy's love for the Mountains, History, and Wildlife of Northwest Montana shows in each of his paintings. Randy, at the age of 12 started his path as an artist, when he first started to paint. He began his professional career in art when he and his wife, Sandy, opened their first gallery in Dayton, Wyoming in 1979. In 1984, with their three daughters, they moved to Eureka, Montana where Randy opened his Studio, The Natural Canvas Art Studio, at their home eight miles northwest of Eureka, in the heart of the Northern Rocky Mountains. From the windows of Randy's studio he can see the aspen trees he uses in his paintings, as well as Douglas Fir, Bull Pine and Spruce. Throughout the winter 250 head of elk frequent the ranch where the McIntyre's raise a small herd of cattle. Moose, mountain lions and bears have wandered through the ranch, and the whitetail deer are in the yard and garden every morning. Randy and Sandy try to spend one day a week hiking in the mountains around Eureka, photographing the landscapes, animals, rocks, tree stumps and anything else that catches Randy's eye, and that he can work into one of his paintings.

Cowboy Therapy

Twilight Calling

Email: naturalcanvasart@yahoo.com

Vickie Flyg

'Number 5'

'Class Picture'

'Packing Out'

Vickie Flyg
2400 Julie Lane
Payette, Idaho 83661

For Show Schedule and Galleries please visit my Website
Website: www.vflyg.com
Email: art@vflyg.com
Phone: (208) 642-4501

'Spring in her Step'

'Running Wild'

'Picking the Way'

'Hunter's Delight'

Working primarily in oil and pencil, Vickie's love of the Western way of life is apparent in her art. Men and women who work with cattle and horses readily relate to her art as she captures the defiant look in the eye of a stubborn horse or the sweet countenance of a newborn calf.

Her paintings and drawings also reflect the admiration she holds for the beauty in nature's wildlife.

Vickie paints what she knows and what is in her heart. To her, a truly successful painting is one that evokes emotion from the viewer in addition to being pleasing to the eye.

Joe Kronenberg

Born in 1968, and residing in beautiful Spirit Lake, Idaho, Joe Kronenberg is a native of the Pacific Northwest. From a young age he has had a love of art. Making a decision in 1988 to pursue a career in sales rather than art was difficult, but something he say's he has no regrets about. "My time away from art has given me a respect for it I never used to have. I also learned some things in the sales industry, such as patience, which has brought my artwork to a whole new level."

A self taught artist, known for his attention to detail and realism he has been known to spend up to 150 hours to complete one graphite drawing and as many as two to three weeks on pastel paintings.

"I don't move on until I achieve what I have pictured in my mind. Even if that means spending an hour or two in the same area of a drawing or painting." As a result of this commitment to detail, often times his work is mistaken for a photograph.

"I still love it when someone thinks one of my drawings or paintings is a photo." Kronenberg takes his own reference photos and combines bits and pieces of a series of picture to achieve his desired result, with western and wildlife being his favorite subjects.

"I put art on the back burner for a long time. Now I am having a blast making up for it. I am very fortunate to have such support from my wife, family and friends. And who could ask for a better place to live as a wildlife artist than North Idaho? I literally get some of my best reference photos out my own back door."

Steer'n and Brake'n - Pastel on Velour

Mama's Boy's - Pastel on Velour

Peyton's Thoughts - Pastel on Velour

Cyra's Christopher - Pastel on Velour

Golden Boy - Pastel on Velour

website: www.kronenbergart.com
email: joe@kronenbergart.com

367 B Summers Road Centralia, Washington 98531 • 360.736.5584

Noodleman

Grange Quilts

My Sisters Garden

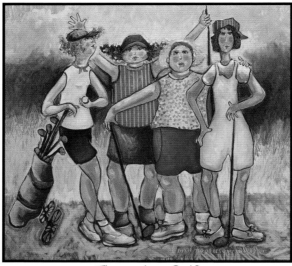

Thursday Golf

The Fort

Purple Feat

Born in Centralia, Washington Dixie began drawing and painting as a child. She is a dedicated-disciplined artist spending many hours creating. A freshness is developed by working in many media. Her whimsical creations are a mixture of realism-fantasy and nature. Oils with strong wild color, of birds, flowers and people young and old.

She and husband Gordon run the business. They have a gallery, office and two studios in their home. They offer at this time some 200 different prints and 60 different cards. Dixie's work is shown in many galleries, gift and frame shops around the United States. She is one of America's native artists.

Elizabeth Ganji

"Horses have always been a large part of my life and it is this subject matter that I find the most inspiring to paint. I make it a personal challenge to capture the serenity, honesty, cadence, and raw energy the horse projects in its presence. I am intrigued by the history of the West and the American cowboy. Together, the horse and cowboy have become patriotic symbols over time, seeming to radiate the freedom and justice our great country was founded upon. The image of the horse itself is indicative of the technique I use in my painting: boldness in the form of color and energy, looseness to encourage freedom and movement, and the suggestion of an untold story that allows the viewer to subjectively discover meaning in the piece.

"My years living in Montana intensified my interest in the West and introduced me to western wildlife such as bears and bison. I went to Montana State University for my Business degree, where I hauled along my two horses and painting palette. Montana looked to me like the most glorious and powerful painting I'd ever seen. It inspired me to start painting full time.

"Recently, I converted to the misunderstood medium of soft pastel. I have found I can achieve a greater depth and moody atmosphere with pastel than with my previous mediums of choice. Once I began experimenting with pastel, I realized I was meant for this medium. Technically, the art of soft pastel is painting with pure pigment held together by minimal binder in the form of sticks. It is this quality that makes the light in my paintings pop with intensity and glow. I enjoy the tactile quality of the sticks, the dryness of the medium and purity of pigment."

Elizabeth is a self-taught painter specializing in soft pastel. She is a fourth-generation artist from a family where the artistic roots run deep. Elizabeth lives with her husband and son in Washington.

Lazy Afternoon II

Sundown At The Upper Deschutes

www.elizabethganji.com

Waiting On The Salmon Run

Deschutes River Bend

Water Media Landscapes by *de l'Aigle*

de l'Aigle was born in New York in 1956. From the age of four, he lived in the West Indies, Spain and Hawaii. In 1970 he moved to Aspen in the Rocky Mountains of Colorado. "It was here that I became intimately acquainted with the extraordinary beauty of the landscape...and let it suffice that words will not do justice here."

He studied fine art in Santa Barbara from 1983 to 1987. de l'Aigle now resides in Northern Idaho. In addition to corporate commissions, his paintings are held in private collections throughout the Netherlands, Spain, Alaska, and from coast to coast in the U.S.

"The subject matter is landscape...but only as a point of departure. I paint from imagination, and the visual/internal experience of just how magical a landscape can be. I sincerely hope to pass on some of this "magic" to the viewer"

The signature for your masterpiece home.

afa
AMERICAN FINE ART COMPANY

Dean Cameron 509-995-9958
www.americanfineartcompany.com

Marcella Rose

Marcella Rose is an award-winning artist whose career spans over three decades. Known for her rich textures, vibrant colors and graceful lines, Marcella's passion for life is reflected in her oil, watercolor, and mixed-media paintings as well as her sculptures.

Marcella is represented by two respected Agents: American Fine Art Company for her Paintings and other Fine Art and ELise Rosenthal for her many licensed products such as rugs, textiles, tabletop, bath accessories, and other home furnishings.

Born in Minnesota, Marcella's career has taken her to Missouri, Arizona and the Pacific Northwest. She now resides in Washington, where she works in her studio by the river, and draws inspiration from her beloved pets and the surrounding nature and wildlife.

The signature for your masterpiece home.

ala

AMERICAN FINE ART COMPANY

Dean Cameron   509-995-9958
www.americanfineartcompany.com

Renee Rigsby

Watercolor painting brings joy and magic to Renée Rigsby's life. It is the perfect medium to capture the vivid colors and brilliant light playing within a scene.

Renée received a minor in art from Washington State University. Her medium of choice for many years was oil and acrylic. Recently she developed a passion for watercolor, studying with well known Northwest watercolorist, Stan Miller.

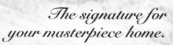

Although she lives in the Inland Northwest, Renee's work has been featured in galleries in Sausalito, CA., Newport, OR., and Spokane, WA. Those who appreciate her work are captivated by the details and colors Renee manages to achieve in each piece, as she seeks to share with others those special moments that have brought her such pleasure.

The signature for your masterpiece home.

afa

AMERICAN FINE ART COMPANY

Dean Cameron 509-995-9958
www.americanfineartcompany.com

Debbie Hughbanks

Debbie is a self-taught artist who shares her home in the wilderness with her husband and a menagerie of animals, both domestic and wild. An artist who works primarily in acrylic or pastel, most often exploring western or animal related themes in her paintings, she regularly participates in regional and national shows and juried competitions. She has been honored to receive numerous prestigious awards and her paintings hang in collections across the United States.

"When a viewer of my art is moved, inspired, or reminded of someone or something important to them, it is the greatest compliment I could ever receive. In my paintings I often try to convey a special feeling or relationship between two or more people, or people and the animals we all share our universe with. I feel that animals are an extremely important part of our existence and should be treasured and celebrated by human beings, and that is what I attempt to do through my art."

The signature for your masterpiece home.

AMERICAN FINE ART COMPANY

Dean Cameron   509-995-9958
www.americanfineartcompany.com

George L. Traicheff

traicheffart@shaw.ca

George is an artist / photographer who has lived from Atlantic to Pacific coasts. He has devoted his life to spending as much time as possible away from civilization, studying, enjoying, photographing and painting the natural world. He prefers to work" en plein air" as much as possible and to use these field sketches and observations as well as his photography to complete larger studio works.

George started drawing as an adult in the mid seventies, (although he had been photographing the natural world since his early teens, with the aspirations of one day being a wildlife photographer.). The art was only a pastime until he attended the international exhibition "ANIMALS IN ART" at the Royal Ontario Museum in Toronto. He was so in awe and impressed by the quality and feeling of the work on view, that this new found energy and emotion, along with artist Terry Shortt, inspired him to pursue becoming an artist. George has been trained in oriental art and studied at the Art Students' League, New York and Ecole des Beaux Arts in Montreal. He has also studied with Clarence Tillenius and the late Robert Lougheed, who have both had a vast influence on George's life and work.

George takes pride in passing on to others what these great artists have taught him, by instructing art classes and workshops. He taught for eight years at the Okanagan Game Farm in Penticton B.C. which is now closed, and taught for eleven years at the Okanagan University College. He has been honored to have students attend his classes & workshops from as far as Japan, England, Mexico, Sweden, Zimbabwe as well as Canada and the U.S.A. His works can be found in private and corporate collections worldwide.

"Feel deeply the beauty of your surroundings and yearn to interpret, to paint them, to make visible to others, through your paintings, the wonder and beauty of the world around them."

Southwest Light

Lazy Day

Serenity

Scarlet September

The Red Bobber

Patience

Megan L. Traicheff

megan.traicheff@gmail.com

Megan is a graduate of the University of Victoria with a Bachelor of Science-Major in Biology degree. She has been a professional artist for most of her life, having started at a very young age and having sold her first work at the age of four. Her first gallery show was held when she was eight years old and sold out in twenty minutes! Since then she has focused on becoming a quality artist, learning all she can about the arts.

Most of her study has come from her father, a professional artist, and at the hands of artist friends who have stayed at the Traicheff household over the years. She has studied art throughout school as well as at the Okanagan Summer School of the Arts. She first started painting with acrylics and then turned to watercolor while studying with Bruce Crawford at his Summerland, BC studio. She has become well versed with various forms of original printmaking and has now turned her focus towards polychromos colored pencils (a very stable, permanent medium) with which she can achieve a wonderful effect. She has devoted her life to the arts and the natural world and is destined for a rewarding career as an artist and biologist.

Megan's career in the arts has been rising rapidly as she has been invited to a number of shows and galleries throughout Canada and the USA.

Her work can be found in corporate and private collections in Canada, the USA, Australia, New Zealand and England.

Panda Falls

Peregrine

That Look

The Stalker

Robert Walton

Robert Walton has recently been admitted to the prestigious Oil Painters of America group. This group, in existence since 1921 was founded for the express reason of presenting realistic paintings to America. It came to light that realism was not being presented to art students at university level and this organization was founded to help give not only the students, but the public knowledge of realism as practiced in Europe and the US. (See oilpaintersofamerica.com).

Robert's experience with realism started at a young age while climbing the mountains of the Northwest. Climbing companions such as the Whitaker brothers (first Americans to conquer Mt. Everest) LeRoy Ritchie, and many others flavored his teen years with thrills, excruciating finger-hanging experiences all encased in the fabulous scenery afforded from Mt. Rainier, Mt. St. Helens, Mt. Baker, Mt. Hood – to all of the major mountain peaks of Washington, Idaho, and British Columbia, Canada. The frosting on Robert's climbing career happened when he was in his 20's and a group of buddies did a first assault on the West Wall of Mt. Rainier (not climbed again since then). A fitting finish to a climbing career that was the starting point for his almost 40 year career painting those same beautiful mountains.

Robert won his first award early in his career at then Puget Sound College in 1974 and since then has gone on to win numerous awards throughout the 10 or so shows he does each year. His inclusion in six galleries in Wyoming, Washington, California, Arizona and Montana have become a showcase for Robert Walton paintings. His web site robertwalton.com is a reflection of all of his current works, including originals, giclees, lithographs and, most recently, a gallery of his sold works from which the occasional commission is forthcoming.

Murals were a huge part of Robert's life up to and including the over 6,000 square foot mural in Heppner, Oregon which was dedicated in the summer of 2005. Click on the word murals in his web site biography to see these. He has been part of many of the Mural In A Day projects in Toppenish, Washington and designed and directed one of those one day miracles. He also has several other murals in Toppenish, Washington that he did entirely by himself.

Leanin' Tree has also been a part of Robert's life since 1989. He has had over 30 images presented by Leanin' Tree Christmas Cards and now is also included in the non-Holiday line with three new birthday cards.

Another Fishing Lesson

Just One More Cup...

Early Snow

Majestic Splendor

Summer Smoke

Noon Stage

Summer Lodges

Mt. Moran

You can visit Robert in his studio in St. John, Washington (64 miles south of Spokane, Washington) by calling him at 1.800.539.2599 (just to be sure he's not out fishin' around somewhere!!). Coffee's always on – come on over and see what's being created!

Apache Crown Dancers (*Left Handed Painting)

Ancestors

Brave Dog Dancer

Into The Light

Home of the Brave One

62   **Gerald Roberts**

Gerald Roberts is a pre-eminent Puget Sound painter whose art is internationally collected. Gerry, a realistic impressionist, uses his extensive art background and what he refers to as "The Gift" to achieve astonishing results and expression in his paintings. His subjects include NuWest and traditional depictions of Native Americans from the past to the present, wild horses in unexpected places, nostalgic scenes, and figure studies. *Due to an injury in 2005 Gerry painted left handed while his right arm healed.

Gerry and his artist wife Norma, who has Lakota roots, live on Whidbey Island in Washington overlooking the Puget Sound shipping lanes. Their travels in the west are usually art research oriented and include the Rockies, the Southwest and the Dakota-Wyoming plains. The "Crazy Horse Monument" in the Black Hills of South Dakota is their favorite location. PowWows are also high on their list to attend.

If you'd like to see more of Gerry's work and a list of his art shows visit his website at www.GeraldRobertsArtist.com. Private showings in Gerry's large studio-gallery can be easily arranged by calling 360.678.3068.

◄ Lone Bear

The Storyteller ►

Wild Horses at Ruby Beach ►

Sandra L. Hiller

www.thesaddletree.net   email: sdltree@aol.com

Sandra, her husband and their daughter live on a small farm in Northeastern Washington. Located three miles from the farm she grew up on. She has had a passion for drawing her whole life, particularly enjoying drawing farm animals and wildlife. Rural farm life provides a never-ending supply of subjects.

Sandra has worked with leather more than twenty years, building harness and tack. She has sold harnesses in countries all over the world, Japan, France and Egypt to name a few. Her experience allowed her to tie together working with leather and her love of art when she learned the technique that she works in today. Sandra's work combines drawing, leather tooling, sculpting and painting in a three dimensional piece of sculptured leather art. Each unique piece is done with one piece of leather from an original drawing.

Packing It Out

Unpainted Backfence Gossip

Brown Trout

Ready For Eight

The Bugler

Pajama Party

Arlene F. Long

"The Fire's Out"

"River Breeze"

"The Boat Club"

PO Box 516 • Clatskanie, Oregon 97016
503.728.2379 • aflong@charter.net

Arlene Feckla (Schlais) Long was born in 1948 in Ketchikan, Alaska. The second child and the only girl to Evard and Feckla Schlais. Her father Evard, of German decent, met her mother Feckla McGlashan while serving in the Coast Guard in Alaska. Her mother Feckla is of Russian and Aleut descent and was born and raised in the Aleutian Islands of Alaska. Arlene grew up along the craggy mountains facing the waters of the Inland Passage that make up Ketchikan, Alaska. As a young woman Arlene came to the "lower 48." She and her husband Richard moved to Northwest Oregon and established a home near the Columbia River in Clatskanie, Oregon. Richard's grandfather, Roy L. Sayre, who was an accomplished naturalist artist and a commercial artist by trade, recognized Arlene's talent in early sketchings she made for her children and proclaimed "If you can sketch you can paint." Thus began Arlene's journey to becoming an artist, painting with oils. After Roy's death Arlene continued to paint on her own, sometimes frustrated with finding the right shade, and "I wasted a lot of paint" she says. Then Arlene learned of a class being instructed by Martha Boentgen, a renowned artist and art professor. Under Martha's tutelage, Arlene developed her skills as an artist. Arlene's work is influenced by the naturalist paintings of Richard's grandfather and her growing up on the water in Ketchikan, Alaska. Water and space are a part of the very fibers of her being and give peace to her mind and substance to her life and her art. Her work captures the scenic beauty of the Pacific Northwest along the lower Columbia River and much of her work contains subjects of historical interest and is reminiscent of an earlier time. Hence the theme of her work "Images in Time."

Prints available from the artist or Hump's Restaurant Gift Shop at Highway 30 and Nehalem Street

Exploring The Wash

Karen Petrovich

Meadview, Arizona • 928.716.6006 • 928.564.2180

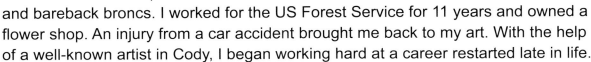

I became interested in art around the age of 14. It was then that I started painting and taking lessons. A move to Wyoming to work on cattle ranches and becoming a big game hunting guide slowed down my art career. I also became a member of the GRA (Girls Rodeo Association) and rode bulls and bareback broncs. I worked for the US Forest Service for 11 years and owned a flower shop. An injury from a car accident brought me back to my art. With the help of a well-known artist in Cody, I began working hard at a career restarted late in life.

My paintings are of my life outdoors; where I visited, worked or hunted. I love painting landscapes. They seem to come together easily for me. I work hard at my art and hope to keep improving. I believe that a part of me comes through on the canvas when I do my art. I have never been one to copy someone else's work. I get excited when I do a painting of a subject that really grabs me. I believe that excitement shows through in my work.

Shell Falls

North Fork Sheep

Grand Canyon Belgian

Erica Curtis
www.ericacurtisart.com

Bridge to Fog

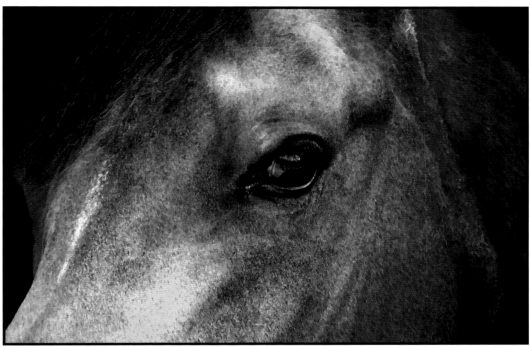

Bay with Flame Stripe

Erica Curtis lives on Puget Island, in the Lower Columbia River. In this beautiful setting, Erica has sought to merge her love of horses, the outdoors and wildlife with her love of photography and art. For more prints, contact and ordering information, please visit her website.

Sunlit Profile

Esther Bartley

503.771.8912 • ARTBYEB@YAHOO.COM

"LILACS AND TULIPS"

"DAINTY BESS ROSE"

"SERENITY"

"FOREST AND DEER"

A native Oregonian, Esther's inspiration comes primarily from her love of the Northwest's natural beauty, which she enjoys capturing in realistic interpretation. Her subject matter ranges from landscapes, seascapes, animals, birds and flowers to portraits and classic cars. Oil paint is her favorite medium.

Since beginning painting in 1971, her paintings have won thirteen Best of Show, many first prizes and other awards in competition at the Portland Fine Arts Guild, The Oregon Society of Artists, Gresham Art Festival, Gladstone Art Festival, Heritage Wine and Art Festival and the Multnomah County Fair.

Many corporate and private collections in the United States, Australia, Canada, England, Germany, Japan and Puerto Rico contain her work. Sixteen of her paintings are available in limited edition prints.

Esther resides in Portland, Oregon with her husband.

Rosalind Philips

Sealion Pup - Galapagos Islands - 1997

Rosalind Philips, photographer, has pursued her love of the outdoors through photography. Inspiration started early in childhood from reading Gerald Durrell's animal travelogues, Ernest Shackleton's journal about the Endurance, and Charles Darwin's Voyage of the Beagle; and from the exploration of nature during family picnics and  at summer camp. Photography was a family activity. Many days were spent learning how to capture the magic of family vacations with the camera. Rosalind began to focus on birds during her teens and has become an avid birdwatcher. Therefore, much of her photography focuses on birds, particularly on the Heron family.

Her photographic adventures are from the Galapagos Islands, Ecquador, Antarctica, Churchill, Canada, Chiapas, Mexico and the United States. You can see more of her work by visiting her website at www.photo-elegance.com.

Penguin Friends - South Georgia Island - 2000

Polar Play - Churchhill Canada - 2003

Great Blue Heron -
Everglades National Park - 2004

Iris Dodge

Iris Dodge (Morgan) was born and raised in Rural Montana. She moved to Alaska and spent 18 years there. She worked on the Alaska Pipeline for several years, as a cook and also as a bookkeeper. It was during the long cold winter months, that she first realized her abilities to put oil on canvas. She says she has always been drawn to the beauty of nature and Gods handy work. The Northwest is very scenic and she feels privileged to have this heritage. She is married to Ron Morgan, has 5 step children and 2 biological children and Numerous Grandchildren. She loves the Lord and is grateful for her talent.

Iris has won many awards including the Grumbacher award, many best of shows, and many purchase awards. She is a member of Oil Painters of America. Her work can be seen in several issues of Art of the West and Wildlife Art magazines. She was published in the First Edition of Notable Artists of the Northwest.

She does a 300 S/N limited edition Christmas card each year. The only edition made of the original is the Christmas card. Her collectors receive the same # each year. Each one of her collectors have the option of purchasing their # of each new painting she paints. One of the most extensive collections in existence, is Chicks Wall of fame in Alder Montana. They also have the total collection of Christmas cards. There is currently a waiting list. There will never be more than 300 in an edition and the numbers only come available if the heirs don't contact her, or if they forget to send a new address when moving. This happens rarely.

Iris does a lot of commission work. She does a quick sketch of her subject in pastels, to get the proper colors, then uses photos and does the painting in her studio on the Alpowa, near Pomeroy, WA. Her paintings can be found in many collections throughout the United States, Canada and abroad.

www.irisdodge.com
E-mail: iris@irisdodge.com
Cell: 208-790-3894

"Red Hat Mama" 12 x 16 Oil
She's a "Red Hat Mama"
from Sheridan, Montana.
She's been called Mama, Grandma,
Sister, Aunt, Friend and Teacher
You'd be hard pressed to call the main feature.
She's a "Yard Sale Junky," found treasures galore,
She's always trying to find someone to mop the floor.
She loves the outdoors and the 4 wheeler is nice,
Each day is a challenge and she'll face it at any price.
You've been a great friend throughout the years,
We've laughed, we've sang, we've shared many tears.
Here's to you, my friend, and this isn't a toast,
but to a long friendship, that I'd like to boast.
Iris Dodge Morgan

"Kentuck" 16 x 20 Oil
Ken Cathey is his real name, but Kelly called him Kentuck,
I don't know why, but the name simply stuck.
He came from the Eastern part of the State,
a business man, he'd surely make.
They bought the Club Bar and Cafe.
The work was hard but it was beginning to pay.
A fire broke out and took it from wall to wall,
but he still had his family, that was most important of all.
He played the guitar and could really sing,
so we formed a band, that was quite the thing.
Vigilantes, we became,
we played our hearts out and earned a little fame.
This was many years ago, and he returns to the valley quite often
With his picture on the wall at Chicks,
ole Kentuck will not be forgotten.
Iris Dodge Morgan

8th Annual Christmas Card

2007 will be the 12th annual Christmas card.
They are all the private collection of the artist
and are all 11 x 14, 9 x 12 or 12 x 16 oils.
Iris Dodge Morgan

"Bethany & Princess" 16 x 18 Oil

Bethany, you are such a delight! Your love of Jesus,
makes your persona so bright.
Your talents are many, you sing like a bird,
may your message of Jesus always be heard.
Iris Dodge Morgan

"Face Off" 11 x 14 Oil

This is what we call it, here in the Old West,
When one of your best friends become a real pest.
They are now teenagers, and probably don't even remember,
the things that upset them when their lives were so tender.
These were pleasant times for friends, parents and grand-
parents alike, Memories we all cherish for the rest of our lives.
Iris Dodge Morgan

ROBERT KROGLE

Robert Krogle, award winning, nationally recognized impressionist painter, instructor and lecturer, brings western, romantic and landscape images to life with broad, confident brush strokes. Up close, his paintings appear to be only an abstract notion, but must also be seen from a distance before they reveal the true character of what he has painted.

Originally from California, Robert now resides in Coeur d' Alene, Idaho where he claims the natural beauty of his surroundings is inspiration enough for his paintings. After four years of education at Chouinard Art Institute of Los Angeles (1966-1970), Robert went right to work, illustrating for the film and recording industries and many fortune 500 companies.

After a successful career as a commercial artist, he discovered a new freedom of self expression as an oil painter. His Best Of Show awards are numerous and he has been selected to paint posters for many of these same events. "It is important that my paintings have significance and purpose beyond a simple graphic representation of what I see. This means capturing the true character of my subject. Fine Art for me is not only a way of self expression, but an exploration of materials, methods and myself, which will undoubtedly result in an ever changing appearance of my work."

"It is my fond hope that my paintings feed the soul, but also inspire people to pursue their own creative interests which will hopefully, in turn, further enrich their lives."

WWW.ROBERTKROGLE.COM

Deian Moore's love of wildlife and nature shines through her art. She has been painting professionally for over 8 years, and portrays elements of her personal, outdoor experiences in nearly every painting. She grew up in North Idaho and moved to Oregon, where she earned her degree in art with a minor in fisheries and wildlife from Oregon State University in 1993. She worked for the U.S. Forest Service for almost 11 years while painting in her spare time. During this period, Deian expanded her knowledge of nature and wildlife, but decided it was time to re-direct her attention to her true passion: painting.

Deian's close attention to detail is very evident in her paintings. She photographs subject material in the field and prepares many sketches before deciding on the final composition. When finished, each piece is an exceptionally rich and meaningful painting that breathes life.

Deian is a signature member of the prestigious Artists for Conservation, an exclusive international society of world-class nature artists. She has won numerous awards and exhibited in several juried shows and galleries throughout the United States. Her work is also in the homes of collectors throughout the West. Deian's rural studio is located in Blodgett, Oregon where she is surrounded by acres of natural beauty. To see more of Deian's work, visit www.deianmoore.com.

Deian Moore Studio

Wildlife and Nature Art

"Painting is my passion! I think half of my love for painting is getting out and experiencing wildlife and nature; even the smallest of creatures excite me when I can observe them in their natural habitat. It's my goal to make an impact in wildlife art so I may give something back to nature."

Christine Meshew

Iris Panels I, II, III, IV

Hydrangea Panels with Fairies

Christine Meshew studied art in high school and college and after a 28-year hiatus began painting again. She has studied under Sharon Hines-Pinion, Deborah Stackowitz, Terry Madden, Val Persoon, and Gale Bennett. Christine has been the featured artist for the Mt. Baker Garden Tour in Seattle and received the Best of Show award during the 2005 Harvest Festival in Bend, Oregon. Her paintings have been shown at the Lakeshore Gallery in Kirkland, Kaewyn Gallery in Bothell, Main Street Gallery in Edmonds, Two Vaults Gallery in Tacoma, and currently at Gallery North in Edmonds. Christine also participated in the Bellevue Art Museum 2005 Art Show. Her clinic, where she practices chiropractic and acupuncture, also serves as her personal art gallery and studio in the Greenlake/Roosevelt district of Seattle.

Christine's earliest childhood memories have always included a fascination at nature's bountiful colors and shapes and how they change constantly with the seasons. Expressing nature on paper is one of the best ways for Christine to use her creative talents to contribute to the world around her. Early art training followed by a career in the healing arts has taught Christine a great deal about self-discovery and how we must all fulfill our full potential and contribute to the world at the same time. Now, during middle age she has literally fallen in love all over again with the wonder of watercolors and the magic of this medium. Christine has made a firm commitment to never set down her brush for too long and will continue the rest of her life expressing God's beauty on paper.

506 NE 65th Street
Seattle, Washington 98115

206.399.9303 · 206.547.3127

www.meshewart.com

Meshew_art@yahoo.com

Lynn Bean

War Pony

Lynn was born and raised in Battle Creek, Michigan, and is an illustration graduate of Kendall School of Design in Grand Rapids. She began her career illustrating fashion, first in Michigan, and then in the San Francisco Bay area.

After earlier years in and about cities, Lynn relocated to beautiful, sparsely populated, west Marin County, California, and eventually to central Oregon's Ochoco Mountains in 1979. In the mountains of central Oregon, life on a remote ranch inspired her to capture the beauty of birds and animals. Many of her first subjects were domestic and wild animals, family cows, horses, pets and wild deer and elk which grace the earlier of her many well-known prints. Much of her later work is inspired by seasonal residence in Meadview, Arizona, where she has produced Native North American and desert wildlife subjects in the grandeur of the Colorado River and Grand Canyon.

International publisher, Gemé Art Inc, lithographed Lynn's early watercolor and ink details. She now publishes her own canvas and watercolor reproductions and a multitude of hand dressed remarques. "Copper Enchantment" was just awarded Top 10 in The Native Art of Horse Painting Competition and replicas of that piece are available. The diversity of her prolific work may be seen at galleries such as Keepers of the Wild Animal Park in Golden Valley, Arizona, Kestrel Winery in Prosser, Washington, and at Lynn Bean Gallery in Sumpter, Oregon. Her many originals, remarques, and prints are also shown at juried art shows throughout the western United States.

Look for Lynn's work also in the Gilbert District Gallery with Dave Bartholet in Seaside, Oregon.

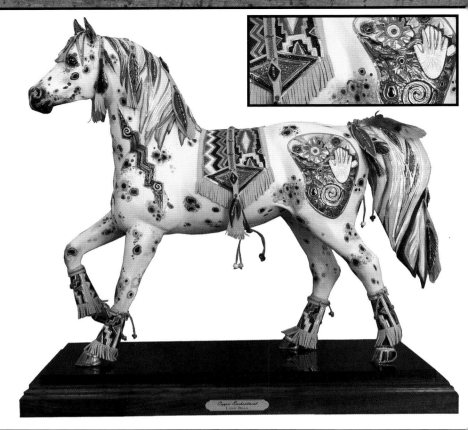

Copper Enchantment

Mare and Colt

Mr. Peacock

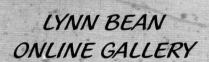

LYNN BEAN ONLINE GALLERY

http://www.lynnbean.com

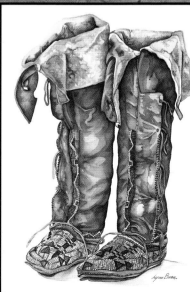

19th Century Arapaho Moccasins

Ede Johnson

509.586.3649 • edejart@msn.com • edejart@aol.com
616 South Conway • Kennewick, Washington 99336

Painting realistically in oils, her pictures project a peaceful atmosphere that is easy to live with. Old buildings, still life, florals and portraits are among her favorite subjects to paint. Serious painting started when she put a set of oils under a Christmas tree with TO MOM FROM SANTA on the tag. Since that time she has won several awards and her paintings are represented in private collections and galleries in the US and abroad. Ede is an art instructor, self taught from an early age. She owned and operated Ede J's Art Studio where some of our Northwest Artists gave seminars and displayed. In 2003 she was honored to be commissioned by the Kennewick Historical Society to paint a 12x15 foot mural for the background depicting the discovery of the ancient bones of the Kennewick Man on the Columbia River in 2001.

Sidney

Indian Summer

Still Life

Lilacs and Decanter

Mom's Helper

Left to Nature

Nancy Acosta — Western - Americana Artist

Nancy Acosta, an award winning artist, combines her love of art and history as she portrays the human spirit through time. She is self taught and has developed her skills in portraits and equine art through hard work and practice, establishing her reputation as an "Americana" oil painting artist. Her work is displayed in many Northwest homes, galleries and at the Collector' Fine Art Shows. Nancy has participated numerous times in Toppenish, Washington's "Mural In A Day." Nancy was the poster artist for the Omak Stampede in Washington, the St. Pau Rodeo and the Umpqua Fishing Derby in Oregon. She has had a number of newspaper articles written about her and has been seen & mentioned in South West Art and Art Of The Wes Magazines. Nancy and her husband, George, purchased Steelhead Run Bed & Breakfast and built a gallery in the spring of '97. Everyone has an open invitation to visit the gallery and Be & Breakfast, it's right on the North Umpqua River in Glide, Oregon on National Scenic Byway 138, the waterfall highway, in route to Crater Lake National Park.

"Head'em Home"

"Cowgirl"

"Cowboy"

"Barrel Racer"

"The Blizzard"

"The Runaway"

"The Crossing"

"Sleepy Time Cowboys"

"America's Most Proud"

"Of One Spirit"

"Sweet Dreams"

"Grandma's Turquoise"

Website: www.steelheadrun.com   Email: acosta_artist@steelheadrun.com
Toll Free Telephone: 800-348-0563

"The Reading Lesson"

"A Nation's Tears"

"Bars & Stars"

"Stars and Stripes"

Companions

Maria Ryan
Contemporary Wildlife Artist

Artist Maria Ryan With Painting

Maria Ryan captures our imagination with an exciting new innovative approach to her paintings of wildlife with a passion. She portrays her subjects in vibrant electrically charged colors in dynamic bold strokes, applied to give dimension and character to each animal. She uses negative space in a magical way to surround her subject with a bold glow of color to balance and imply dimensional space. Light, form and shadow also play an important part in each painting's design and composition. The eyes of each subject are painted realistically to make each animal have a soul and communicate an emotional connection to the viewer. Every new painting is a surprise. Her dynamic contemporary approach is not mere representation, but a unique, powerful and exciting vision of each subject – WITH PIZAZZ!

She feels the most important functions of a painting are to be a feast for the eyes and to elicit the viewer's emotion. Each new work brings more excitement and inspiration for her next painting. A guiding quote by Oscar Wilde is framed on her studio wall: "No great artist ever sees things as they really are. If he did, he would cease to be an artist."

Long Rangers

4850 West Deer Path Trail • Coeur d'Alene, ID 83814-8697
208.667.9490 • Fax: 208.667.5530 • e-mail: mariaryanart@verizon.net

Charlene Monger

Charlene was born and raised in Everett, Washington and now resides in the beautiful Methow Valley. She grew up with a love for horses and would constantly draw them. Her parents always encouraged her art. Then her sixth grade teacher took notice of her horse art and arranged her very first show at school. Fifteen works of art displayed where all could see them! Charlene was so surprised on removal day to see her classmates lined up to ask for one of her pieces of art. She had given them all away. That's when Charlene realized for the first time that people not only enjoyed her art but wanted it.

A dream came true for Charlene when her parents gave her a horse on her 14th Birthday. Now, she could ride a horse as well as paint them.

Her art work was interrupted when she married and had children. Later she resumed painting and drawing. But now, instead of painting horses she was doing seascapes and still-life paintings for Clubs of Edmonds and Firdale Galleries. Her heart was really in horses and landscapes though, and she was able to return to those subjects in the early seventies. It was her Native American husband who inspired her to study the Plains tribes and include them in her horse paintings. A big plus for her as he would often model for her. Thus, some thirty years later she is still painting horses, Native Peoples, and landscapes. Charlene's art has been in shows such as The Toppenish Western Art Show, C.M. Russell Auction, The Fred Oldfield Western and Wildlife Art Show, Omak Western & Native Art Show, Ellensburg National Art Show & Auction, plus numerous others.

High Plains Scouts

![Five Indian Horses]
Five Indian Horses

Whispering Winds Studio
PO Box 513
Twisp, Washington 98856

www.charlenemonger.com

The Hunter

![Methow Valley Winter]
Methow Valley Winter

Four Indian Horses

Chris E. Huffman •www.sundownmetalart.com•

Sundown Metal Art is a small business that introduces you to the next generation of metal art by transforming metal into its true and purest form. All items are completely custom made on a to-order basis and handcrafted to perfection personally by Chris Huffman and his wife, Tracy.

Chris and Tracy were both born and raised in rural farming communities in Eastern Oregon. They enjoy working with animals and being outside. Chris and Tracy worked on several cattle ranches and farmed when they were growing up.

Through Chris' experiences ranching and rodeoing, and with the help of Tracy, he captures passion in his artwork. Chris' interest in art began at a very young age. He has experience in handcrafting artist pieces from wood, leather, stained glass, painting and metal. Chris' real passion is working with metal.

Tracy has a background working in western retail and is an artist in her own right. She enjoys helping Chris come up with new ideas for his passion. Chris relies on Tracy to help promote his work to the world.

Chris and Tracy moved to Hermiston, Oregon where Chris became employed for the Hermiston Police Department. They have been very fortunate to have four wonderful children that inspire them to continue working and creating artwork for you to enjoy. The family is very involved in several youth originations both at the state level as well as nationally.

In 1998 Chris started to become more serious about delving into his interest in art to help with the stress of being a police officer. Through the support and belief in Chris's artwork Tracy convinced Chris to enter pieces in the local county fair. Tracy talked Chris into doing art shows throughout the Pacific Northwest. Tracy convinced Chris to start a small business and now Sundown Metal Art is featured in businesses and private homes in several different countries throughout the world.

Since 1998, Chris and Tracy have gone from mainly doing flat pieces of art to full three dimensional art pieces and are always trying to improve their artwork.

To my wife, Tracy, I do not know how to thank you enough for the support and love you have shown me. To the people that have enjoyed my artwork, thank you so much and I hope I will continue to make things that will impress you. Sincerely, Chris

3D Trees and Horses

3D Grapes

4 Foot Circle - "Jan's Love"

3D Lifesize Horse Head "Guardian"

3D Elk Piece

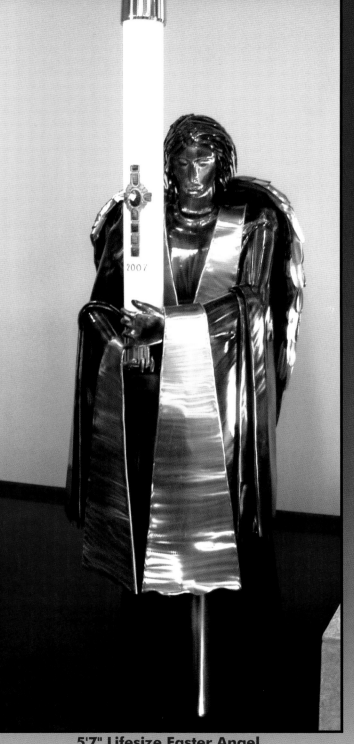

5'7" Lifesize Easter Angel

Ranch Sign

3D Metal Antler Lamp

3D Metal Wall Scape

Cowboy Patriot

Round Up

The Funeral

Anita Palmer, Olney, Texas, is an internationally acclaimed award-winning artist. Her paintings hang in congressional offices in Washington, D. C., Austin, TX, and other valued collections. Mrs. Palmer's art has also been featured on the covers of magazines and CD's. Anita's awards have been numerous at prestigious juried art shows, often winning Best of Show and People's Choice. When viewing Anita Palmer's art, rural Texas and the West are the prevailing subject matter with horses and cowboys dominating the theme.

From before starting school in her birthplace of Altus, OK, Anita Smith (Palmer) was drawing and painting using her mother's discarded art supplies. At seven years of age, she won her first national art show with a crayon drawing of a dog looking at a lizard, which toured the United States for four years. From an early age a preponderant artistic skill was evident in her ability to capture realism on a two dimensional surface.

After many years of begging for art lessons, Anita, at age eleven, began studying with Ruby Belinti, an accomplished Oklahoma artist. While in college at Southwestern Oklahoma State University, she minored in art, later returning to complete an art major. These studies provided a broad base of art appreciation, from china painting to abstract art. It was not until she went back to her love of painting people and animals in their natural prairie environment that Anita Palmer found her real niche.

Tammy Bridges

6335 Mount Vista • Helena, Montana 59602
406.457.0087 • www.montanafarmart.com

Sanchez

Lil' Roper

Lil' Roper

Lil' Roper

Born in Missoula, Montana, artist Tammy Bridges now resides in Helena. Tammy and her husband Marc share their spread west of Helena participating in a variety of outdoor activities.

After several years of building and woodworking, Tammy turned her creativity to metal fabrication. She completed a welding course at Helena School of Technology in 2002.

Tammy has developed a passion for art focusing on materials found representing ranch/farm life from the past. Through her creativity, she breathes life into the rusted and worn-out iron. Her placement and welding of the materials that consists of parts from plows, cultivators, seeders, balers, mowing machines and spike tooth harrows creates a second life for the iron pieces as they are entwined to depict a variety of western and animal characters.

Since she works full-time, Tammy's art is done primarily on weekends. Several weekends and evenings are also dedicated to hunting for the old time materials she needs for her metal sculptures.

Goose Planter

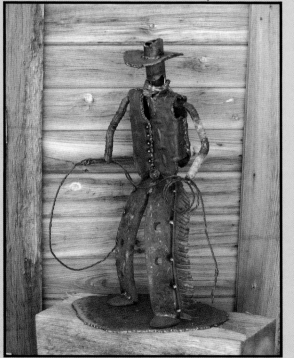

Working Cowboy

Indian Chief

Moon and Star

Marysville Sun

Patricia T. Cooper
"P.T. Cooper"

PO Box 3133 • Pasco, Washington 99302
Home: (509) 547-2018 • Cell: 509-845-5585
Email: pcooper2018@charter.net

What motivates me as an artist is the need to visually express what I see in the world around me and in the world inside my head. The difficulty lies in slowing my imagination enough to focus on one expression at a time.

My photography and artwork reflect an interest in history, such as the American Civil War, my Japanese American heritage, nature, people in action, costuming, and in my flights of fantasy. Portraying the Civil War in art evolved from my late husband's and my participation in re-enactments in the Pacific Northwest. Taking part in science fiction/fantasy, historical gaming, and Japanese anime conventions and exhibiting in their art shows has created a market for my work as well as providing me with the camaraderie of creative graphic artists, musicians, authors, costumers, and dancers.

The Washington events in which I currently participate include the Western Art Show in Toppenish, the Street Painting Festival in Prosser, and the Tri-Cities science fiction/fantasy convention art show (Radcon). My work may be found in private collections in and outside of the United States.

I am grateful to my parents, Eddie and Seiko Edamatsu, and to my late husband, Bill, for supporting and encouraging my creativity and individuality.

Just Before The Battle, Mother

Lady Warrior

Good Evening Felicity

Obon Dancers

Harbinger

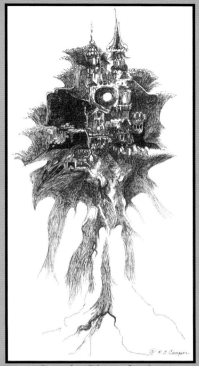

Castle Singularity

Khamsin

Wind Swept

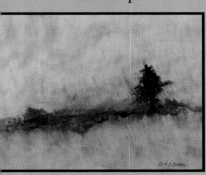

Through The Mist

Through Enemy Lines

Cooper Self Portrait

Duke Collage

DAVE BARTHOLET

www.davebartholet.com   Email: bartholet@theoregonshore.com

"Silent Night"

"Chickadees"

"Day Ridge Bull"

"Wild and Free"

PO Box 920
Seaside, Oregon 97138
503.738.4222

Dave, a self taught artist, was born in Tacoma, Washington in 1949. Having a childhood in the wilds of Wyoming, his love for wildlife was founded early on. In 1971 he started his journey as a professional artist selling through galleries and to private collectors (mostly sympathetic relatives) bless them all! In the early 80's Dave ventured into the world of show business, participating in juried art shows mostly in the western U.S. His loose style of watercolors have proven to be very popular with collectors, as he estimates his works to be in nearly 100,000 households, and have been sold in hundreds of galleries worldwide. Besides being a spokesman for wildlife awareness issues, he avidly supports wildlife conservation groups throughout the country. It is his belief that he was born to paint and that he doesn't just do it because he can but because he must.

Dave, an avid outdoorsman, spends his spare time hunting, fishing and filming wildlife throughout the west. Today he lives with his wife, Penny, in Seaside, Oregon, where they are co-owners and operators of The Gilbert District Gallery.

"Summer Daze"

"Clash of the Titans"

"Gold Finches"

Kristi M. Stone
Western Artist

I live with my husband, Dan, in Redmond, Central Oregon High Desert, raising Corriente roping cattle. Calving season, weaning and branding. Snow, wind, frozen water tanks, sagebrush and junipers. Money could not replace any of it. I do my art because I enjoy it.

"I can't imagine myself not being able to be surrounded by beautiful desert, our horses, our dogs and our cattle. Sharing this with my husband, who has provided me with the opportunity to spend my time doing what I enjoy, I am blessed. I am blessed to be able to live where I love it, do what I love to do and share that with people through my art."

"Golden Morning"　　　　Oil

"Fringes"　　　　Pen & Ink

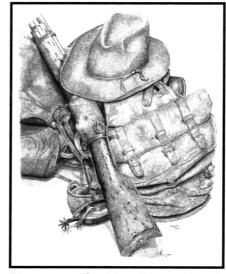

"Preserve The West"　Pen & Ink

"McDermott Bronc #544"　　Oil

"Clarno Barn"　　　　Oil

"Tim"　　　　Oil

Check out either of Kristi's websites at:
www.diamond-s-quartercircle.com
or
www.krististoneartist.com

"Wisdom of the Past"

"Trick Me Once"

"Elk Spirit"

"Ancient Waters"

Pati Deuter

605.943.5600   email: deuter2ravens@venturecomm.net

"Silent Star Sight"

Pati Deuter grew up in Los Alamos, New Mexico, which is just above Santa Fe. The spirit of the Southwest is reflected in her works.

Pati owned and operated a gallery in Mesilla New Mexico and another in Cedaredge Colorado. She moved to Ree Heights, South Dakota with her husband Jim in 1997, where they both maintain working studios.

Pati defines her watercolors as visionary art . She uses a combination of cubism and realism to create a unique style. She says "I have a whimsical disregard for what is expected and strive to surprise myself and the viewer with original ideas."

www.patideuter.com

Sallie A. Zydek

Big Horn Ram, 1995   Scratch board

First Alert, 2005   Scratch board & Stipple

Pride of The Prairie, 1995   Acrylic

Cougar, 2005   Scratch board

My techniques include acrylic painting, India Ink stippling and scratch board, which are used individually and together, to produce highly detailed images of nature's textures. Habitats range from deserts and high plains to wetlands, rainforests and ice fields, with subjects displaying the translucent scales, soft 'feeling' fur and/or individual feathers of a biologically appropriate species. I try to express the 'soul' within each of my wildlife subjects, which is most visible to me in the glistening of their eyes.

Acrylics in reds, oranges and translucent washes with the subject in silhouette are favored design elements. "Pride of the Plains" uses such tones to draw the viewer's eye from the near thunderclouds to the subject and then back to the darker details of the more distant sky in the background of the painting.

I am currently working in black and white, using stipple and scratch board in combination, due to the extremely fine level of detail both of these mediums allow. Stippling, with a Rapidograph pen produces the series of fine dots on both Bristol Board and scratch board. Etching is done with scratch knives to produce images by removing material from 'Essdee Scraper Board' and 'Clayboard.' Many times I use both methods to complete a picture, depicting the individual hairs of an animal in scratch board with details of the foliage done in stipple. The combination allows a delicate, yet dramatic look and intricate texture, at the cost of being a highly unforgiving work medium. These techniques produce extremely detailed images which take from 200 to over 800 hours to produce. I enjoy the subtle depths I can achieve in using both these mediums, combining detailed bright highlights with absolute black and whites, to form edges in which the subject contrasts with, yet blends into it's environment.

The choice of specific tools, supplies and techniques depends upon how the subject matter affects me emotionally at the time I decide to produce the image, and how that impression is to be conveyed to the viewer.

I am a member of Artists for Conservation/ Worldwide Nature Artists Group and involved with the "Ft Worden Wildlife and Nature Art Exposition" (once called the "Pacific Rim Art Show") now held annually, the First Week in October, at Fort Worden, Port Townsend, Washington.

11817 242nd Ave Ct E • Buckley, Washington 98321
(360) 889-0094
salliezydek@comcast.net

Coming At You

Have You Heard

Hunters

Old Huckleberry Bunkhouse

Chris Gunter

The world I create with my art is the world in which I would want to live. It has the sleepiness that life used to have, that we have lost in all the fastness we are forced to live in now. I couldn't live without art, I have to do it, look at it and be around others who do it.

I was born in the uppermost corner of the fat part of Idaho 50 miles from the west entrance to Yellowstone park and 60 miles from Jackson Hole Wyoming, an area surrounded by history. My mother sparked my interest in history with the local stories of Pierre's Hole, the mountain men, the fur rich upper snake river valley and the local Native Americans. My father worked in the woods and would help with the muscle and movement of wildlife. I was drawing mule deer before I could write. I had a picture of Santa's sleigh being pulled by mule deer which was submitted by my first grade teacher to the local newspaper and ended up on the front page of the paper.

Every summer of my early childhood my sisters and I would live in an old sheepherders camper in the woods, while my dad sprayed D.D.T. for the rocky mountain timber beetle and logged. In our part of Idaho there were only dirt roads and trails, so we used pack horses to get into the areas where my dad was working. He would put us kids on top of the soup cans (kind of like riding a camel) giving us a birds eye view of the wildlife and beauty in this untouched wilderness. Few people had viewed these areas and fewer still could even imagine the untouched and undisturbed quality of the area around Ashton Idaho; you couldn't help but become some kind of artist, you just had to be.

For samples of my current work and upcoming shows please email me at lostidahoan@hotmail.com or write Gunter Fine Arts, E360 Cedar Street, Belfair, Washington 98528.

Hannele Gauthier

Creating art has always been a life-long pursuit for Hannele Gauthier, a recognized Northwest Artist. Hannele offers a diverse uniqueness, whether her art is portrayed in the abstract or realistic styles. Hannele's illustrations create a means in the investigations of life itself. By enhancing a desire to comprehend the nature and boundary of her identity, she draws from the connections of values that define who she is as an individual.

Hannele, a very talented and self-taught illustrator, has always enjoyed the challenges in creating art. As she strives to captivate the beauty of the moment, she ignites her creativity and passion, which defines her artistic images.

Even though Hannele's main focus is portraits, she has been known to generate other types of art; whether it be hand-rendered or digitally enhanced. She does not limit herself to only one style, medium, or technique. She feels by doing so would be like looking down a very long tunnel with no room for expansion; with the obvious limitations for the abundance of explorations in the artist's world.

Amazingly though, an illustration from Hannele will ensure that the emotions captured in her works, will, ultimately, result in a lasting treasure forever.

Linnie - 9" x 12"

Contented - 12" x 16"

Autumn Harvest - 14" x 18"

Hey You Don't Say ~ 15" x 15"

Herbie My Luv ~ 9" x 12"

Deep In Thought ~ 15" x 15"

She Who Watches ~ 16" x 20"

King's Carmen ~ 9" x 12"

Selah ~ 2" x 8"

"To have someone admire what one has done is the highest compliment."

◄ *Oregon Coast*

Aerial View of Mt. Hood ►

Instructional workshops may be scheduled upon request.

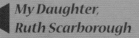

◄ *My Daughter, Ruth Scarborough*

Mt. Hood Sunset

Living in the beautiful northwest has certainly been the motivating factor in Betty's desire to capture the natural scenes that surround her. After several years away from the Puget Sound area, she is home and will finally be able to focus on her art work again. Looking out across the vast body of water in front of her home is both tranquil and inspiring where a new studio is just being completed for her to have the best creative atmosphere for her work. She can hardly wait to move into the new studio to put on canvas all the new ideas that are waiting to fly from her mind onto canvas. As new work is completed, she will be posting it on her website.

Betty's experience covers a wide spectrum of Fine Arts. She is an Artist, Instructor, Author and Gallery Owner which gave her the opportunity to represent other artists. She has traveled throughout the Northwest and Alaska teaching and showing her work and doing shows. What the future holds is creating new work, new styles, new techniques and new shows and galleries to show her work.

Betty has published two instructional books; "Northwest Scenes" and "Palette Knife & Brush Impressions." The books provide studies from which to work, Step by step instructions, a color palette and techniques are included in each book. Her books can be ordered by phone, (360-608-2140) or through her website (northwestartwork.com).

To visit her studio, please call 360-860-0077

Iris ▶

Favorite Jeans

Synnove Pettersen

Synnove was born in Norway and moved to Canada with her family. She studied at the Art Center College of Design in Los Angeles on scholarship.

Her next stop was Mexico where she exhibited with a group of artists called the "Clique Ajijic" and had many successful solo shows. Back in the USA, Synnove continued to hone her skills with workshops and classes as well as teaching art. She works in pastel, acrylic and oil. Her distinctive style is clear and pleasing—reflecting affection and sensitivity for her subjects. She has collectors in the United States, Canada, Europe and Mexico.

Synnove now draws inspiration from the beauty of the Pacific Northwest and shares her joy for life through her paintings.

Contact Synnove for commissions in any subject and medium:
telephone: **360.426.9798**
email: synnove99@gmail.com
website: www.synnovefineart.com

Deep Forest

Thistle

The Knapps

Soaring Eagle

Hooped Earrings

Joy Descoteaux

"John Fredricks"

"Antique Barrels"

Joy Descoteaux, a New Hampshire native, now lives in Oregon. Her mediums are oils or soft pastels and she uses them to create still lifes, landscapes and figurative work. Now that she is near the Oregon coast, she has added seascapes to her subject matter.

When Joy sees something that strikes an emotional chord within her, her intent is to recreate the feeling and share that emotion with the viewers of her work. In this way her realistic work reflects her impression of the subject matter.

Joy's award winning work has been exhibited in art shows and galleries throughout New England as well as in Oregon and has been purchased by business organizations and art collectors as well as by the general public. Her work can be seen in private homes as far away as England and Australia.

Commissioned work is generally accepted. You can see more of Joy's work on her website, artwithjoy.com and contact her by email at fineart@artwithjoy.com. Joy asks that you put the word "art" in the subject line to assure avoiding her spam folder.

"Beach Baby #8"

"Catnap"

"Three On The Beach"

"Traveling Man"

FLY FISHERMAN

NORTH HEAD LIGHTHOUSE

BLUE RIBBON MULE

MULES AT THE ROCK CORRAL

Eugene,
Oregon

541.344.0069

email:
tmaddoxart@aol.com

THE MONARCHS

TERRY MADDOX

541.344.0069

WWW.TERRYMADDOX.COM

Terry was raised on a ranch out of Jacksonville, Oregon. He drew as a youngster under an alladin lamp - no electricity and didn't start his art career until October of 1975, at the age of 42.

His style is totally self-taught and he has had no art training of any kind. His drawings are very realistic but very soft. His subject matter varies greatly, primarily of the great outdoors. Terry individually water color tints his prints to create beautiful realistic images that can be considered water color tint originals.

He has been in the 'Top 100' of the National Parks - 'Art in the Parks' twice in the four times he entered. He does art shows throughout the west and has been 'Best of Show' on numerous occasions.

He has portrayed his art career around a 30 year math, science and PE career as well as a varsity baseball coach at Springfield High in Springfield, Oregon.

He played several years of pro baseball around a stint in the US Army. In college he was named to the 1957 All-American baseball team while playing for the University of Oregon. He was inducted into the University of Oregon Athletic Hall of Fame in November of 2006. He has a BS and MS in geology at the University of Oregon.

HIGH DESERT BARN

Watercolors by JoSaki

Jo Iwasaki Masker

I have always been fascinated with watercolor paintings. I love the wet, uncontrolled, self-mixing of colors that create the most wonderful effects. I am intrigued by the free flowing expression achieved with just color and water. This medium is conducive to my style of being loose, spontaneous and intuitive. Especially since I like to paint out of my head, often I never know what's going to come out.

Self taught, I have dabbled with watercolor for the past 10 years and sell originals, prints and cards through art shows and festivals. I enjoy trying new mediums, techniques and subject matter. Recently I have been experimenting with acrylics, collage, porcelain and encaustic.

I have the pleasure of sharing my experiences and acquired knowledge by teaching a watercolor painting class at a local community college and elementary kids after school. I also teach at my home studio. I believe anyone can paint and that I can bring out the artist within. Paint with joy and pleasure!

Wet Blooms

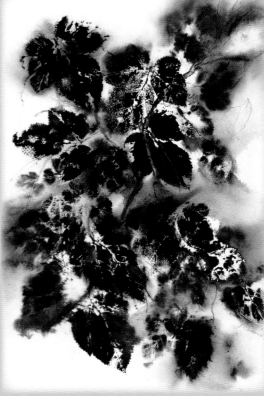

Blackberry Leaves

Loose Lily

Just Flowers

Follow Me

www.watercolorsbyjosaki.com
email: JoSaki@comcast.net

上先

Carrie Glenn, born in 1980, grew up traveling across the U.S. with her family, often changing locations yearly. She has lived all over the U.S. from the East coast, (Virginia) to the West coast (California) and everywhere in between having moved well over 20 times and counting. After many years of continued traveling across the U.S. and even some international travel, she has returned to her native state, Oregon. Carrie is currently producing art in her home-based studio in the Portland area with her husband and family. It was clear at a very young age that Carrie was born gifted with an artistic talent, as she has had no formal training. As a child, she spent hours upon hours developing her gift of painting and portrait skills. Carrie has a rare ability not only to create amazing life-like details in her work but also to capture the true emotion and depth found in her artwork. Carrie's unique creative skills led her to develop a realistic technique, often using mixed media, which has become her trademark. Her portraits are often mistaken for photographs.

Carrie maintains a partnership with the March of Dimes, Portland, Oregon Chapter. She donates artwork annually to bring in top dollars for their "Signature Chef Auction." Her artwork has also been shown and donated with the March of Dimes, Seattle, Washington Chapter's, "Celebrity Chef Auction" to help raise awareness for March of Dimes and their charitable efforts. Her work has been juried into numerous art shows throughout the NW such as the "Ocean Shores Fine Art show" and the "Lake Oswego Festival of Arts." She has won many awards for her outstanding artwork, including the "Honorable Mention Award" from renowned Professor and artist, Robert Feasly. She has also been commissioned for corporate artwork and public installations for entities such as "London Fog," "Horizon Air" and "Thomasville Furniture." Her work can be found in such reproductions as canvas prints, signed prints, posters, calendars, cards and collectable coffee mugs. Carrie's commissioned artwork can be found Internationally. Some of her new artistic ventures include working on illustrating and coauthoring several children's books and introducing her artwork into the film industry. Her future plans include relocating with her family to Southern California.

Louie Armstrong

First Tree

Color Floats

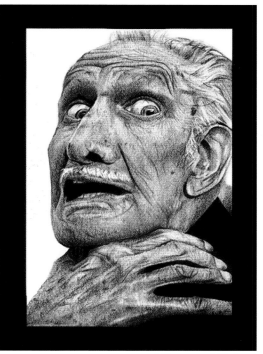

Vincent Price

www.carrieglennstudios.com
Email: carrie@carrieglennstudios.com

introducing...
Fred R. Meyer

Fred Meyer was born in Detroit, Michigan in 1936. Deemed by those who know him as a "true left brain thinker," Fred was destined to be an artist. After the structured life of a formal education, Fred hopped cargo planes across South America ending up in Jamaica where the lifestyle and people influenced a great deal of his earlier work.

Upon returning to the United States, his Dad said, "Get a Job!" Fred opened a Multi Media Commercial Art Studio and prospered until his retirement in 2003. Following his son to the North Coast of Oregon, Fred has once again focused his creative side into his current works, specifically the fine arts medium. He credits the easygoing lifestyle of the coast as a major force that has lead to his current works...the rain helps too.

Fred works best in the morning and mainly when it's overcast and rainy and the sun is not beckoning him outdoors instead. He does not burden his work with any complex analysis or high-flown commentary; he simply feels that his work communicates to each person differently, that you feel something!

"Buy art for you and not for an investment... leave that to the art investors."

I've done thousands of pieces of art in the advertising business. I've seen all kinds of art from pinks, blues and wicker in Florida to lobster traps and sea shacks in Maine.

Now on the Upper Left Edge, I've seen many Haystack Rock pieces...

I've done pieces for others...be it Corporations, Investors or Projects. This current grouping was done for me. In considering my works, please do not buy to match your couch or fit that needed blank wall in the hallway...but for the feelings it generates in you.

Frederic R. Meyer

503.436.2573

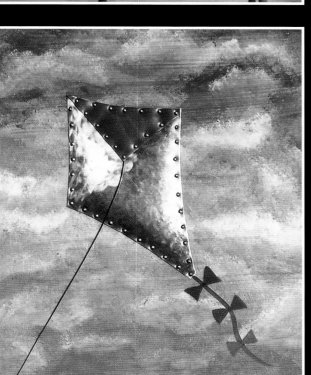

Jean Fritts

509.697.4348 • jbhuck@compwrx.com

Jean Fritts was born as a twin and the youngest of six sisters. She was born in Everett, Washington and raised in the Yakima Valley in Washington. Thirty-four years ago she moved to Selah, Washington, a small community at the foothills of the Cascade Mountains. Jean has always loved art. She began oil painting twenty-five years ago and has found her place in Old Master Style.

God is a big part of her life and influences her greatly. She thanks the Lord for this artistic gift that He has blessed her with. Another important influence in her life is her large family which includes: her husband, eight children, twelve grandchildren and ten great-grandchildren. This is seen by her use of many of them as characters in her artwork. Her other "family" are her two Pomeranians, which reflect her love for animals. Along with this love for animals comes a passion for nature. She even has a cabin nestled in the mountains where she constantly goes to relax, study nature and paint. Currently, she teaches oil painting at the senior citizen center, where she shares her knowledge and love of art.

The Visitor

Deer Creek

Solitude

Down Pour on City Life

Little Thunder

Diane Greenwood

In painting after painting, artist Diane Greenwood embraces the exhilaration of Montana. Born in the tiny town of Sidney, Montana, Diane grew up a true western farm kid, tending to the animals and thriving on the vast sky and flat fields surrounding her. A move to Billings in 1980 led her to an enduring love affair with the contrast of mountains and moving water found in nearby Yellowstone Park. She has never lost the wonder of the beauty surrounding her and continues to visit favorite places, setting up her easel to capture the beauty of the picturesque landscape around her.

Diane has been creating art for twenty-five years, working in oils, pastels, and photography. She is greatly influenced by such native artists as Clyde Aspevig and Tim Shinabarger. Diane has received numerous awards and recognition for her artwork. She is a member of the Western Heritage Artists Association, an Associate member of the Oil Painters of America, as well as the Pastel Society of the Northern Rockies.

Diane teaches and paints at her gallery at 412 North Broadway, Suite 11, in Red Lodge, Montana. She is represented by Common Grounds Gallery and Nature's Wonders Fine Art Gallery in Red Lodge, Montana as well as participates in numerous regional and national gallery shows. Her fascination and love for capturing some of the grandeur around her is a driving force in her life and work.

Aspen Glow

Shoshone Country

www.dianegreenwood.com

Her Majesty

Bull Elk

LINDA M. PHILLIPS

Linda is an award winning artist and shows in art shows throughout the Northwest and throughout the United States. She has shown in The American Academy of Equine Arts in Lexington Kentucky, Western Spirit Art Show in Cheyenne Wyoming, St Paul Rodeo Art Show in St. Paul Oregon, Alamo Kiwanis Art Show in Texas and the renowned Phippen Museum Western Art Show in Prescott Arizona.

Linda belongs to the Western Heritage Artists Association, Western Artists Association and the Women Artist of the West.

12 Hours Old

phillipspaints53@hotmail.com
Hermiston, Oregon
1-541-720-0688

Watch My Back

Ropers

Jordan Valley Corral

Christopher B. Mooney

www.christopherbmooney.com
email: mooneycb@hevanet.com

Christopher Mooney is an accomplished artist who paints urban landscapes filled with all the moods of city life. His large oils on canvas are often based on views of the many Portland bridges. Mooney's compositions of bridges are anything but ordinary. He paints them from an unusual point of view giving them a dramatic perspective which makes them both realistic and abstract at the same time. Light plays an important role in Mooney's paintings, illuminating the structure of the bridges, casting shadows and making you look at the bridges differently than you had before. Portland, Oregon is a city of rivers and bridges. Mooney's fascination is with how the geometric shapes of the bridge's steel girders frame the landscape of the city. Mooney also paints bridges from other places in Oregon and beyond.

Burnside Bridge

Broadway Bridge

Christopher Mooney's works may also be viewed
in The Rental and Sales Gallery
at the Portland Art Museum in Portland, Oregon.

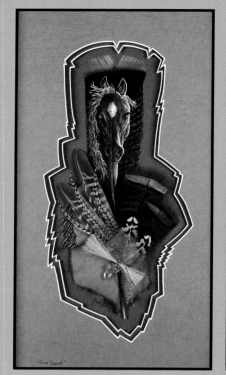

Sunspirit

Nightsong

Little Hummer

Janet LeRoy

Original Artwork on Feathers

Born in Denver, Colorado and raised in Southern California, Janet always loved to draw and work with her hands. Although Janet has had no formal art training, she began pursuing art as a career in the mid 80's when, she began entering small art and craft shows in and around the San Bernadino Mountain area of Southern California with handmade items such as decorative baskets and leather carvings.

She discovered painting in the early 90's after she moved with husband, Steve, to Breckenridge, Colorado. The majestic mountains and abundant wildlife in Colorado inspired Janet to paint the animals and scenery she so loved. Looking to express herself in a truly unique way, Janet began painting on feathers and this new art form soon became an obsession.

Janet decided to mount and frame her painted feathers, adding a complimenting arrangement, using deerskin, smaller feathers of varying shape and color, a variety of semi-precious gems, crystals and other items that add to the mood of the painting.

Painted Pony

Tatanka

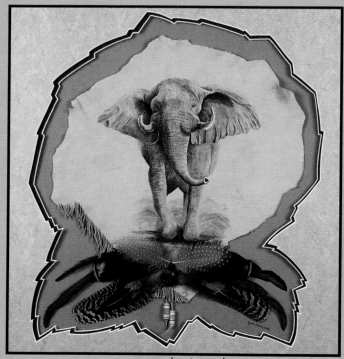

Dust and Thunder

Silvertip

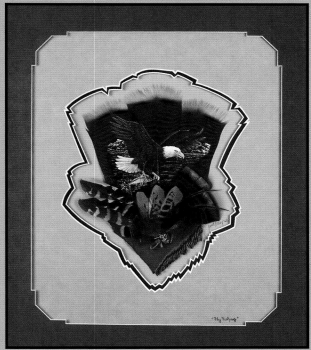

Flyfishing

In order to create an original mat style, Janet enlisted Steve's help. Together, they mastered the art of hand carving the mat to match the shape of the feather and arrangement.

Janet and Steve have traveled the west since 1993, participating in art shows and festivals, where Janet has received numerous awards. Recently, they purchased a small ranch in Hotchkiss, Colorado where they now reside with their four horses, two dogs, Scarlet Macaw and eight turkeys. Along with Janet's father, they have also opened a gallery, studio and frame shop in the middle of town, aptly named "Birds of a Feather."

They thoroughly enjoy meeting the people who collect their work and they make regular donations to various wildlife preservation and other non-profit groups. Limited edition prints of their work are also available.

P.O. Box 673
Hotchkiss, Colorado 81419

www.janetleroy.com

Proud and Free

Freeflight

SUSAN SWAPP

Foxes

Having been raised in the Pacific Northwest, Sue has a deep appreciation for the beauty and majesty of nature. She has always felt a close affinity with the nature and animal life found in the area and elsewhere.

Sue's art portrays a moment of time in the private life of animals or captures the beauty of nature in its' majesty or plant life in it's precise individual beauty.

Sue paints in both oil and watercolor in a style using fine detail for a realistic representation. Her work is in private collections throughout the United States, Canada and Europe.

Sue's work is available as originals, various types and sizes of prints, and cards, through various art groups, at numerous venue displays, at Seabear's in Anacortes, and at the Blue Heron Gallery in Coupeville.

Winter Waters

New Horizon

Expectation

Joe Watkins has taken the art of feather painting to a higher level with his talent for design and painting as well as his unique hat cutting and sense of presentation.

Using wildlife and Native American imagery, he attempts to convey a sense of majesty and power in each individual subject. While primarily interested in creating artwork that appeals to the public, he also works to preserve a sense of what was or is rapidly disappearing.

The creative process starts with a pencil sketch of the general design and shape. For large works a mylar template is made from sketches, one for the form of the feathers and one for the subject. The templates are used as stencils to determine placement of the subject on the feathers. After selecting the feathers and gluing them in place, they are sprayed with an acrylic sealer to preserve and stabilize them. The spray also creates a surface that holds the acrylic paint. Once the template is used for placement, the images can be rendered. He then hand cuts a mat design to fit each individual work and creates a "shadow box" effect using foam core to separate the face piece from the basic mat.

Joe studied art with various local teachers in his hometown in central Utah while growing up and became a draftsman before joining the U. S. Air Force in the late 1960's. Once in the military, his artistic talent became apparent and he worked as an illustrator/artist for 21 years until retiring in 1989. During that time, he studied painting and sculpture with several well-known German artists. Being an illustrator contributed to his emphasis on design and presentation in his current works. After employment in a Salt lake City ad agency, he decided to follow his dream and has been a full time artist for the past 10 years.

His artwork is in collections throughout the world. Among the owners of his work are Sir harry Tuzo, former Aide De Camp to Queen Elizabeth, Mr. Gregory "pappy" Boington, Mr. Stansfield Turner and Former Secretary of State Alexander M. Haig. His works are regularly purchased by the Rocky Mountain Elk foundation, Ducks Unlimited, Pheasants Forever, and the Rocky Mountain Mule Deer Foundation. A number of galleries in the western U.S. purchase his artwork.

Joe and his wife currently reside in a small community in the mountains of northern Utah.

Joe L. Watkins

PO Box 193 • Morgan, Utah 84050 • (801)-829-3683
www.jwatkins-art.com • email: jwatkins48@hotmail.com

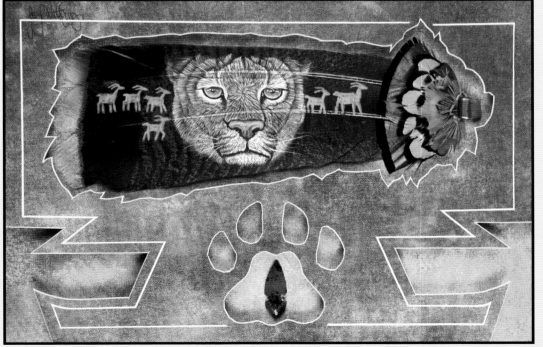

C. M. HUNT
WESTERN ARTIST

1419 South Winter Road
Spokane, Washington 99212
509.924.6780

Artist Charles Marion Hunt was born on September 15, 1934 in a tiny log cabin in Arkansas. Two years later the Hunt family moved to Surprise, Arizona and placed the artist in the grand west that he would grow to love and depict in his paintings.

With no opportunities for formal art schooling, Charles could only rely on his talent, the Arizona landscape and studying the works of Russel, Remington and Leigh to guide his self teaching for his western paintings. Studies of works by European masters in France and Germany also helped him to develop his mixing of impression and realistic styling.

Mr. Hunt paints the "Romantic West" and always endeavors to illustrate strong moods with ideal story matter. His paintings are forcefully rendered with a unique handling of strong lighting, deep shadows and rich colors.

"New Country"

"The High Trail"

"Early Start"

The Monarch"

"Desert Nocturne"

"Back From Mexico"

Peter K. Mathios

website: www.mathiosstudios.net

email: peter@mathiosstudios.net

541.812.0358

"With acrylic paints and brushes, my passion is to capture the art that I find in the everyday moments of nature."

Reflections - Black Necked Stilts

Lessons

Red - Bellied Woodpecker

Sunlit Sanctuary

Lisa Stout

www.AardvarkMemories.com   DearLisa@AardvarkMemories.com

Lisa Stout's bursting palette of post-impressionist paintings showcase compelling images that range from portrayals of strong women in deep contemplation to primitive renderings of domesticated wildlife. Wanderlust from age 18, until her recent retirement from her career as an airline captain, Stout now finds she rarely ventures from the Pacific Northwest's Olympic Peninsula where she focuses her authentic energy as an artist and writer. A compilation of her work may be viewed at www.AardvarkMemories.com

"Woman Reclining With Mia"

"Enchanted Way"

"Global Warning"

"8 Months"

Gary Holland

Shining Mountain Gallery is located 35 miles north of Yellowstone Park at 1390 East River Road in the town of Pray and features Gary's artwork plus fine arts and crafts of over 40 other artisans. Open year round or by appointment, call 406-333-4704 or email us at shiningart@wispwest.net.

Anticipation

The Gift

Gray Wolf

Gary's passion for painting started as a young boy in his hometown, Williamsport, Maryland. His work in art has ebbed and flowed over the years. Fifteen years ago, after many visits to the area visiting an old friend, and later moving his brother to Great Falls, Gary made Paradise Valley, Montana, his home.

Since then, Gary has been devoted to his artwork. Subject matter focuses on Native American culture which he feels a special affinity for, perhaps because his grandmother is full-blooded Seneca. Inspired by the beauty of the mountains, rivers, and wide-open spaces that is 'Montana,' he paints the wildlife and western scenes that are so near.

Twelve years ago, Gary met Vicky. She was on a summer hiatus from her work as a real estate agent in Bellevue, Washington. Touched by Gary's artwork, her energy and marketing expertise soon launched them both into the world of art. After taking Gary's art class in 1996, Vicky discovered that she really did have a functioning right brain and has managed to develop her own loyal art following.

In 1999, they purchased the Old Pray Bar, and the following year began construction on a beautiful gallery that is attached to the historic old bar. In 2001, Shining Mountain Gallery opened and is a delight to all those discovering this 'art oasis' in the middle of Paradise Valley.

Spirit Flower

When I Grow Up

Native Trout

Night Before The Hunt

Buffalo Frost

Anna Mae Lindsey

"This is not a complete representation of my work," says artist Anna Mae Lindsey. Her paintings reflect family values, memories and the beauty that can only come from having experienced life. Having lived in the desert and in the mountains of Colorado and in the green hills of Oregon, Anna's paintings reflect the beauty of nature.

Anna comments, "I decide which medium will work best for each student, then I do a series of the subject. I do historical subjects and houses, wildlife and western, landscapes of Northwest scenery, people, seascapes and still life. I study, experiment, take lots of photos and do many sketches." She adds, "I am constantly learning, there is so much to discover and paint in this beautiful world that God created."

Anna is a member of the National Museum of Women in the Arts, Society of Washington Artists, Portland Fine Arts Guild, and North Clackamas Guild. She teaches oils, acrylics, watercolor, pastels and pencil. From the age of 5, her talent has been awarded. She has continued to paint and study ever since.

Anna sells from galleries, various juried shows, exhibits and by commission. She has held numerous offices and chaired many programs connected with fine art. Anna is a published artist and was featured in The Artist's Magazine (1996).

Clear Lake

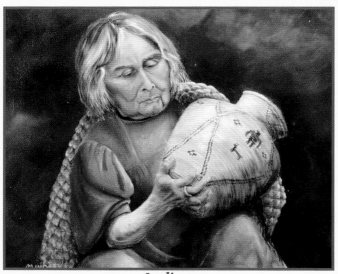
Indian

Fisherman

Anna Paints!

Anna Mae Lindsey
Contact Information

Phone: 503-668-4476
Fax: 503-668-6646

Email: annapaints2@wwjv.net

PO Box 502 Sandy, Oregon 97055
39161 SE Rude Road Sandy, Oregon 97055

Hidden Valley

Fragrant Path

Summer Time

Angel

GARY LOVE
PHOTOGRAPHY

Gary Loves Passion for landscape photography began on a camping trip when he was teenager. Taking photographs became a way to share his adventures and love of nature with friends and family. Gary has been taking pictures as an amateur photographer for over 15 year ut in 2005 after selling his landscape design company he became a full-time professional photographer. " I think having a landscape esign company has really given me an edge as a photographer. I was at a young age able to create a layout for a property that achieved a alance and harmony that I also strive for in the composition of my images."

Gary breaks many traditional photography rules because he has no formal training; however, this is something he feels is to his benef gained what knowledge I could from the books I read, but quickly realized I learned much more by keeping a log of each photo taken, en reviewing those notes while looking at each piece of film. I think that in landscape photography each person needs to see and xperience nature's ever-changing beauty in their own way."

Love spends months on the back-roads of America armed with just his cameras and camping gear. "I usually remain at a location for a reat deal of time before picking up my camera, exploring and getting a sense of my surroundings." In early 2007 Gary embarked on a ful me exploration of first, the U.S., then the world, in an attempt to capture the once in a lifetime moments that have become an essential ement to the images he is most noted for in the art world.

Gary Love's photographs document his painstaking attention to detail and also his ability to see the perfect compositions presented by other Nature. His images have been featured in several publications; his work is collected by various corporations as well as individual ollectors all over the world, and is available in numerous fine art galleries. His patience and dedication to his craft pays off.

"Built To Last" Wyoming

"Purple Haze" Washington

"I genuinely respect the sacred trust that nature photographers have with their subject matter, to portray no more than what was actually before their lens at the time of the shot. Nothing more-nothing less."

Gary Love

"Soulshine" California

"Thousands of tired, nerve-shaken, over-civilized people are beginning to find out that going to the mountain is going home; that wildness is necessity; that mountain parks and reservations are useful not only as fountains of timber and irrigating rivers, but as fountains of life."

John Muir

"Simple Twist Of Fate" Arizona

"Born To Run" Wyoming

Gary Love 123

" Like a Rolling Stone" Montana

"Powder Your Face With Sunshine" Oregon

"Free Fallin" Oregon

124 Gary Love

"Bright Side Of The Road"   Oregon

"Long As I Can See The Light"   Washington

"Into The Great Wide Open"   Idaho

Lynn LaRose

"I love the American West...and my paintings reflect this desire to portray the spirit of the people from our past and present; the American Indian, the cowboy, the mountain man. Getting to know my models, their tribe and background, is a must as it reflects in the eyes and the spirit that projects from the canvas."

Originally from Alabama, Lynn LaRose moved to Texas in 1990. After a trip to Arizona and New Mexico to view the American Indian art galleries, she was inspired to learn more about the culture and history. Her oil paintings and pencil work reveal her love for the people and faces of the deep south and the southwest.

Art showings include the Colorado and Texas Indian Markets that are held once a year in Denver, Colorado and Arlington, Texas. Her artwork is also displayed at Visual Expressions Gallery in Cedar Hill, Texas.

Lynn is a member of the Ellis County Art Association and resides in Waxahachie, Texas with her husband Larry and daughter Worth.

Victory Flag

J. Lewis

Waiting for the Long Knives

www.laroseart.com
website

lynn@laroseart.com
email

972.567.0241
phone

Rustler's Brew

Brave Journey

Penne Erler-Boyd

503.738.7864

Penne Erler-Boyd is a graphic artist, copywriter, novelist, playwright, fashion designer, a colorist, musician, composer, lyricist and sometimes a nut. After a successful career as a graphic designer in Portland, Oregon, she went back to Cannon Beach where she'd spent summers for most of her life. There her paintings began to take off at DragonFire Gallery.

Her love of shadows, spotted sunlight, special effects and transparent little girls became her hallmark-places from her childhood with beauty and magic. The subjects she painted had light radiating off hair or sparkling water in creeks and seed fluffs floating in the air.

"The painting of my sister is at the age of puberty. It's a magical time in a girl's life and was a photo take at a little creek near the entrance to Ecola Park."

She also paints her popular "Mushroom People" series. Their oval, grayish heads have realistic, piercing eyes and slashes for mouths with a row of sharp little pearls for teeth. Even though cute-they usually make social commentary.

"Magic happens when you really get into the subject of your painting then magic comes and surprises you."

Game of Life

Spring Magic

Memories of Childhood Past

Judgement Day

Wini's Girl

My Dream

Karen Lucas

PO Box 889 • Graham, Washington 98338

Color is the word that comes to mind when you look at Karen's artwork. It is the driving force and the binding element to her painting no matter if it is watercolor, acrylics, oils or any combination of mediums or subjects.

She began her career in 1979 and traveled and participated in art shows all over the western states for years. Her artwork continues to be a collectable commodity.

She now lives and operates a gallery at the base of Mt. Rainier in Graham, Washington. Promoter, artist, teacher, wife, mother and grandmother are all words to describe Karen.

Desert Blooms

To see more
of Karen's art
or for
commissions,
go to
www.lucasart.net

Golden Moment

Jocelyn is an avid outdoor and wildlife enthusiast. From an early age, her frequent family trips to the mountains afforded her the hands-on experiences of nature and kindled her desire to pursue her childhood passion of being an artist. Through unlimited support of family and friends, she has flourished in the opportunities of the art world and her dedication to research has taken her to many destinations, including Costa Rica, Alaska, Patagonia and her undeniably favorite... Africa. She has attained international recognition for her paintings and sculptures both, and enjoys the versatility of tackling many subjects and mediums to keep her inspirations alive.

MOLLY KUBISTA

PO Box 66 • Terrebonne, Oregon 97760
541.383.0823 • Email: sales@indiandreamstrading.com

Molly Kubista is a member of the Samish Tribe of Washington State. Born in Seattle and raised in Liquid Sunshine, she perfected her style of horses for which she is known for. Whimsical and at time humorous they also contain power and movement, but her work is diversified doing also jewelry, old style beadwork and painting. Her work reflects the history of her native people specializing in the style of the 1800s. Molly's work has been purchased from around the globe including Germany, France, Hong Kong, Australia, England, Austria, Netherlands, Africa, Sweden and all of the United States. Molly has shown and sold at the following: Smithsonian, Heard Museum, Portland Art Museum, Fort Vancouver, Museum of Natural History, High Desert Museum, Tamastslikt Institute, Oregon Historical Society, Santa Fe Indian market, Indian Art Northwest, Hibiwing Center, Museum at Warm Springs and has won many awards for her work. So take home a piece of history in the making by Molly Kubista.

PEACE UPON MY LIPS ▶

◀ **MODERN AGE**

NEGOTIATIONS ▼

◀ **PEACEMAKER**

WITH THE WIND ▶

Julie Malcom

Pendleton, Oregon   email: jamalcom@uci.net
(541) 379-1920

I love the old ways of life. That's why I embrace the Western theme in my work, the spirit of raw strength and survival that built our unique American history out of the frontier dust. I'm from Pendleton Oregon, the home of the Pendleton Round-Up rodeo. Here I can paint themes that I see daily but speak to me of the West's true spirit, of lives spent on horseback, of the closeness mankind has with animals and the land. One of my portrait paintings is in the Round-Up's Hall of Fame.

This drive to capture the world in which I grew up has been deep in my soul since my teenage years when I first realized that I could be-and would be-an artist. At age 18 I visited France, experiencing the wealth of art there. For years I drew, did pen and ink renderings, and learned watercolor before raising our four children. They're older now so it is time to paint! My studio where I devote myself to oil painting is on a river in an old building that resembles a castle. When I open my studio door I feel that life too has opened new doors for me, and look forward to seeing and painting everything yet to come.

△ Chief

◁ Cowboy

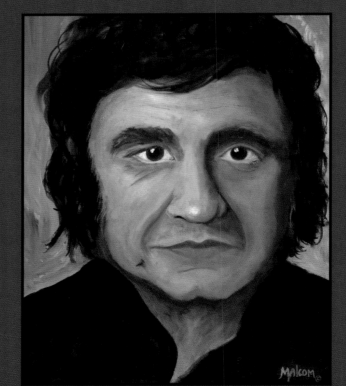

△ Cash

Gunslinger ▷

Deb Owens

www.dj-arts.com
email: debsart@gorge.net

Born and raised in New Mexico, Deb Owens moved to Washington state's Columbia River Gorge area in '79. Deb states, "It's quite different from the southwest region but just as beautiful." Deb, who is a self-taught artist, first started drawing at the age of 7. She started oils in '67 and later discovered pastels. Deb describes pastels as "wonderful, spontaneous, direct and forgiving." Deb started painting various subjects of southwest culture, mostly people, animals, wildlife and landscapes, because each personality is different and each painting is a new challenge.

Deb likes to experiment with different mediums other than pastels such as acrylics, watercolors and watercolor pencils. She also painted on ornaments, leather, tree conchs and old crosscut saw blades.

Most of Deb's works are commissioned. Her paintings have been exhibited in several competition shows and have won numerous awards from the Society of Washington Artists, county fairs and solo shows.

Also, Deb has participated in Artists of the Gorge exhibitions. Deb is a new member of the Northwest Pastel Society. She has recently started painting again full-time and looks forward to entering some of the art shows around the states. Her care and attention to detail is evident in the many paintings already on display.

One of her favorite quotes is "When the Spirit does not work with the hand, there is no art." -Leonardo da Vinci

Ivan

Day Dreaming

In The Mist

Up Close & Personal

Suzi Q.

R. Stem

www.rstem.com

1628 East Second Street • Deer Park, Wa. 99006
(509) 276-6966
Email: rwstem@yahoo.com

At The Tree Line

The Cowboy

Roosevelt Beach

Four Seconds Flat

Gordon Pass

Redfish Creek

View Robert Stem's works at the following galleries

Big Fork Art & Cultural Ctr. Big Fork, Montana	Wagon Wheel Drummond, Montana	A. Hooker's Gallery Great Falls, Montana	Rouge Blanc Gallery Newberg, Oregon

Ranch Horse

Four of a Kind

Susan Neill

www.susanneill.com

Leather n' Denim

Self-taught artist, Susan Neill's passion for animals, horses in particular, began at an early age in St. Paul, Minn. Spending many of her waking hours at the stable, the sounds, sights and smells of those surroundings created many of her happiest childhood memories. Susan began drawing when she was very young and continued into her early teen years. Naturally, the subject matter almost always included horses or other animals. As time passed she found less and less time to devote to drawing. The fast pace of normal life followed by raising a family along with a career as a banker perpetuated a 25-year hiatus from her art. Susan continued as an avid horsewoman and was drawn to the competitive nature of the show ring riding cowhorses.

In 1997, with the encouragement from her husband John, Susan began drawing again. Amazingly enough her choice of subject matter had not changed much through the years. In 2002 Susan decided to venture out of her "safety zone" that was the very controllable medium of charcoal and begin her journey into the world of watercolor. Having been around horses all of her life the desire to recreate them on paper remained strong. These subjects, along with her love of all things western, are portrayed in much of her work.

Susan lets her "senses" lead her to these subjects that she loves to paint. For her there's nothing like the smell of saddle leather, horse barns, and fresh cut hay......nothing as soothing to the ear as the hoof beats of horses or the bawling of cattle in the early morning......nothing more serene than watching a herd of horses peacefully grazing or more enticing than a pile of rusty branding irons. Susan's painting allows her to escape to a place filled with nothing but the things she loves.

Susan now resides in Southern California with her husband John and best friends, Australian Cattle Dog "Bailey" and Golden Retriever "Max." She is an associate member of "Women Artists of the West" and the "American Academy of Women Artists." Her work can be seen at shows throughout the western United States. Susan's paintings have been featured in "Equine Vision-Horses in Art" and "Western Horseman" magazines.

DAVID KRON

David's love for art has always been a part of his life. Showing great promise at an early age. He was born in Portland, Oregon and has called Oregon his home state all his life. He has lived on the Northern Oregon coast for 37 years, residing in the Cannon Beach, Seaside area. Pastels have been his passionate preference for his northwest depictions of land and sea. The complementary color structure that David uses, creates harmonious, exciting colors, evoking expressive emotions.

MOUNTAIN LAKE

HAYSTOCK ROCK

LONE TREE

DKRONARTS@YAHOO.COM
503.738.0755

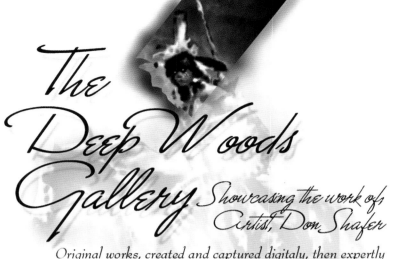

The Deep Woods Gallery

Showcasing the work of, Artist, Don Shafer

Original works, created and captured digitaly, then expertly
printed to capture the escents of each subject.
The image known as Storm Horse, is shown in the background.

Please take a few moments
and visit my web gallery at
thedeepwoodsgallery.com.
I sincerely hope you enjoy my work.
Don Shafer

Email Don directly at
thedeepwoodsgallery@yahoo.com
or don_shfr@yahoo.com

JAMES R. BECHTEL
Fine Art Photography

Artist Jim Bechtel
and Guinness

Jim, originally from Michigan, has been a photographer for 40 years. He spent almost a month every year photographing the west. It's scenery, wildlife and history captivated the artist for some time and in 1998 he moved to Emigrant, Montana to make it his home and formed Natural Graphics as a vehicle for his work.

Jim's works today has evolved to a masterful mix of film and digital technology as seen through his discerning eye. As one of the few still shooting large format, which includes both 4 x 5 and 8 x 10 formats along with 35mm and medium formats, he enjoys capturing what he laughingly refers to as the big picture. As owner of Color Premier, one of the finest Fine Art reproduction facilities in the West, Jim's work is then moved to digital via drum scanning and then artistically mastered and rendered on canvas or similar fine art materials. All phases involved in the preparation of the artwork are done by the artist.

In the early days Jim was a sporting event photographer covering primarily boat, car and Grandprix racing in the midwest. Then he discovered the intimacy of photographing wildlife and realized that was going to be his path of choice. This evolution naturally drove his eventual move to the west where today he still actively can be found hiking with camera in hand looking for that special scene or moment.

Bull Moose in Hoare Fros

Yellowstone Falls

Paradise Valley Board of Directors

Tatanka

Heron Preening

Stowe Vermont

Electric Peak

Twin Lakes / Yellowstone Park

Jim Bechtel
198 East River Road
Emigrant, MT 59027
406-848-7550

Contact electronically at either:

Natural Graphics
info@natrlgraphics.com
www.natrlgraphics.com

or

Color Premier
info@colorpremier.com
www.colorpremier.com

Wranglers

Spurs

Oxbow Bend

Rocky McGinnis

Rocky McGinnis lives on Orcas Island in the San Juan Islands with his wife Lynn and two daughters, Kalie and Chelsie.

I find a lot of enjoyment in Art of all Styles. Nature and wildlife have always meant something special to me. I hope the Eagles I carve bring enjoyment to all others who see them.

I would like to say a special thanks to all my family and friends who through their help and support and suggestions make my art better then if it was just coming from me alone. If anyone would like to contact me or my wife Lynn, you can e-mail us at rocksplace@hotmail.com It would be our pleasure to speak with you. The eagles are carved out of many different species of wood.

◀ Palangi

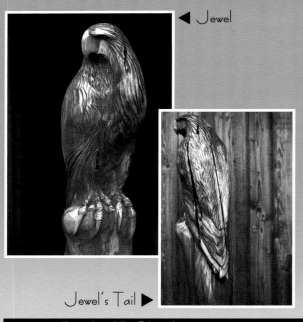

▲ Angel Restless

◀ Jewel

▲ Palangi Talons

Jewel's Tail ▶

◀ Songbird

▲ Red Tail Angel

▲ Restless

Rafiki Mufasa ▶

SHIRLEY HACKETT

2220 W. Cleveland Avenue • Spokane, Washington 99205

Shirley Hackett is an award-winning plein-aire' artist whose work has been exhibited throughout the west. She is largely self-taught and has attended workshops with various well-known artists, in addition to drawing classes at Eastern Washington University. In addition to this book, Shirley is also featured in "Northwest Artists," a coffee table book with over 150 Northwest artists featured in it.

"Roozengarden Tulips"

"Spokane River Walk"

"Soft Light at Midday"

She has received several awards, including the 2002 Producer's Award at the Western Art Show in Spokane, Washington, the 1998 Best of Medium Art Show at the Snake River Showcase, and 1st place at the Salmon River Exhibition in 1995.

Hackett finds her inspiration by traveling to numerous places, camping and painting on location, and capturing the grandeur of the mountains and the intense hues of the desert-like areas of central Washington. Her vibrant paintings portray an emotional response to what she sees.

509.328.5649
509.230.7467
srhackett@icehouse.net

"Windy Columbia River"

"Stormy Sunrise, Hope"

Julie Van Sant

Julie was raised in Colorado, and attended the University of Colorado with a minor in art. She always hoped to make a living by expressing her creativity, while staying in the mountains. In 1972, she left the Rockies of Colorado and headed for the continental divide of New Mexico. She worked in several different mediums, but it was in Santa Fe that she had the chance to train with top silversmiths, and she knew she had found her life direction in silverwork. The flavor of the southwest, as well as the spirituality of native cultures, helped to mold her style. A move to Montana over twelve years ago opened yet another door to design inspiration. Her love of the west, southwest and northwest, continues to influence her work.

"My desire is to create jewelry that is infused with emotion and spirit. Customers often say my pieces are their favorites, and they wear them daily. Their feelings fulfill my mission for the jewelry to be of high quality, styling, and durability, with the comfort to be worn for a lifetime." Julie specializes in custom fit bracelets, but also makes buckles, rings, bolos, necklaces, and much more. Catalogs are available upon request.

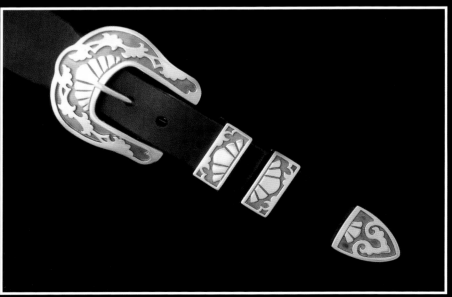

Sterling "Vines" Tipset Buckle

Sterling and Turquoise "Scroll" Buckle

Sterling Trout Buckle

Lapis, Sugilite, Gold and Sterling Bracelet

Sterling Turquoise Bracelets

Turquoise, Jade, Gold and Sterling Necklace

Turquoise, Coral, Agate and Sterling Necklace

**Julie Van Sant
Custom Jewelry
PO Box 827
Kila, Montana 59920
www.julievansant.com
Email: julievs@hotmail.com**

Melissa S. Cole

4917 N Boeing Road, Spokane, WA 99206
p#(509) 535-3489 e-mail-sirenagraphics@hotmail.com

Artist Melissa Cole often finds herself snorkeling with salmon, smooching manatees, and swimming with tiger sharks. It is from these amazing encounters that she derives much of her inspiration for her vividly colored, heavily textured and patterned acrylic paintings.

Cole was born in Oregon and raised in London, Hong Kong, and India. She graduated from Oregon State University with a degree in Zoology and spent time as a naturalist guide in Mexico. She's written over 30 children's natural history books and travels with her usband, who is a wildlife photographer specializing in marine fe. Melissa has always dabbled in art, but has spent the last even years fully devoted to it. She is strongly influenced by thnic patterns, which she sees in her travels abroad. "You'll nd lots of dots, and a distinct border pattern in each of my ieces." Her work is found in galleries ranging from Stephan ine Arts in Anchorage, Alaska to The Wild Side Gallery in Key Vest, Florida.

When she isn't waterlogged, Cole finds her oasis in the outhwest. The colors of the rock, the strangely shaped egetation, and fascinating wildlife provide added interest for er artwork.

"No matter what subject I paint, my style is consistent, lthough it is almost always nature that draws me in."

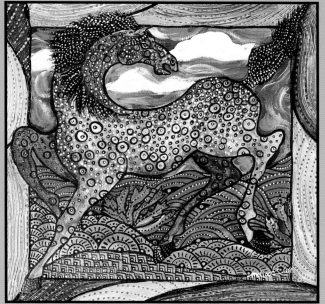

Dancing In The Desert

Tide Pool Heron

Chicachile

Kingcrow

Electric Trout

www.melissacole.com

Lee Johnson
Wildlife Artist

Lee Johnson is a native of a farming community in northern Minnesota where Johnson and his father and brothers enjoyed many hours of hunting and fishing. Many farms in this area have at least a few wooded acres where a variety of animals will make themselves at home and several lakes in close proximity provide excellent fishing. Johnson has observed the cycle of life of many of the North American creatures and he enjoys reproducing those familiar creatures in oil on canvas and very often more than one critter can be found interacting with the main character.

Johnson has participated in many art shows, festivals and auctions in Minnesota, Texas, Alaska and the state of Washington. Johnson's artwork has been presented and acknowledged in such prestigious programs as the Washington State Duck Stamp Competition, the Federal Duck Stamp Awards program as well as an extended showing in the Legislative Building in Olympia, Washington.

Pond Side Gathering

www.leejohnsonwildlifeart.com

Raccoon and Frog

Eyes of the Wolf

Mountain Lake

Eagle

Paul Langston

Paul Langston is a talented Northwest artist who uses a variety of mediums including oils, watercolors, wood burning and woodcarving. A mostly self-taught artist, Paul's work reflects his avid interests in old barns, lighthouses and rural landscapes. Over the years, Paul has been involved in art clubs, art shows and art classes from various artists.

11814 SE 321st Pl
Auburn, Washington 98092

253-939-0820

email: Langston01@comcast.net

Bass Harbor Head Light

Lake Scene At The Cascades

Montana Farm Scene

Summer Garden

Heceta Head Lighthouse

Shannon M. Fharnham

Shannon M. Fharnham is a bronze artist from the Methow Valley, in the North Cascades of central Washington State, where she has lived since 2001. Having been raised on a horse and cattle ranch, she is an accomplished horseman and holds two college degrees, one in agriculture and one in travel.

Shannon started sculpting at 18 years of age and is completely self-taught. She worked briefly in a bronze foundry, wax carving, as a way of learning the process of casting bronze sculpture. Her work is initially done in a pasteline (oil-based) clay or foundry wax and then is taken to a foundry to be cast in bronze. She utilizes aspects of nature in her work, using rocks, tree limbs and other things in nature to achieve realistic detail in her wildlife sculptures.

In the Methow Valley she shows her work at the Confluence Gallery in Twisp, Washington and the Winthrop Gallery in Winthrop, Washington.

She has shown in 2006 and 2007 in the Wenatchee Art Walk in Wenatchee, Washington. She was awarded the Best Three-Dimensional prize at the Omak Western Art Show in 2004 & 2006.

She shows her work at various locations around Oregon and Washington and on the web at Methow Arts Alliance.

Naptime - Approx. 3/4 Lifesize

River Play - Lifesize

Best Friends - 12" x 8" x 7"

Fharnham Bronze
Twisp, WA
(509) 997-2220

www.MethowValleyArts.org

Fishing Rights - 12" x 8" x 10"

Margo Fox
FOXDEN STUDIO

Margo has been drawing and painting most of her life, and her style and techniques are primarily self-taught. She has developed her own unique style with oils. Many of her paintings are landscapes and wildlife, which reflect her love of nature and the outdoors. Some of the landscapes are dichromatic, using only black and white. They are heavily textured, with many layers of oils to detail the raw power of light and dark in nature. Margo and her family always try to fit in hiking, camping, and backpacking into their vacation plans each year. She says she will never be without inspiration as long as she can visit God's great outdoors.

Margo began marketing her original paintings professionally in 1994, with the support and encouragement of her husband and best friend Larry, and their daughter Niccole.

Her work is sold at art shows, Foxden Studio or by commission. Contact Margo for information at 509-547-3845.

699 Curlew Lane
Burbank, WA 99323

foxden@columbiainet.com

Sunflower

Sun Geese

Glacier Lake

Mountain Lakes

High Lakes

The Past

Glacier Trail

Ron Adamson

Final Flight

If you can not stop to see Ron's art work at an art exhibit you can see it on the web at www.ronadamson.com or you can see video's of Ron's work on Youtube just type in Ron Adamson on the search line.

Growing up in the remote part of northwest Montana on the banks of the Kootenai River was inspirational. Ron started his interest in wood carving as a small child collecting drift wood and watching the wild life along the Kootenai. His artistic pursuits started in 1973 with a half semester of art in High School.

To sell paintings in a small northwest town in Montana was virtually impossible so the next step for a young man in a lumber town was to apply for a job in the lumber mill. Ron's interest in wood led him to learn to grade lumber. In the environment of a lumber mill Ron started to carve on wood during his one hour lunch and on break times.

From the banks of the Kootenai River Ron had kept a collection of cotton wood bark and soon became adept at carving western figures into the rustic pieces of wood. The lumber mill environment helped Ron develop the ability to carve fast and in front of people. That was a crucial development as in the following years while exhibiting at art shows Ron could take part in the "Quick Draws". Ron was the first wood carver to be able to complete a wood carving in the short time allowed for a quick draw and have it presentable for auction. Ron's first art exhibits were sell outs. As a surprised young artist, Ron said "People were buying my wood carvings as fast as I could make them and ordering more! Tourists were buying my small Indian wood carvings and taking them home to Europe, Japan, Australia, New Zealand, South Africa and even South America, within a couple of years I had my sculptures in every continent except Antarctica."

In the late 70's Ron began experimenting with bronze sculpture and was soon winning awards and selling his bronze sculptures through out the US. In 1995 Ron won the Kinney Wildlife Award in Ellensburg Washington for a set of Canada Geese. Ron's sculptures have been accepted in the CM Russell Art Show and Auction since the late 1970's and the Spokane Art Show as well as the Celebration of Western Art in Puyallup, Washington where Ron has won best of show for Sculpture 8 times.

Ron was the first artist in North America to have and create his own web page. That opened up the way for Ron's art to make it to Hollywood. Ron was selected back in the late 1990's by the Posada Foundation to sculpt a standing man from the "Eagles" song "Take it Easy." The six foot tall sculpture was placed as a focal point in the town of Winslow Arizona.

In 2003 Ron was chosen to sculpt awards for the Reno Film Festival. The first year of the Festival was dedicated to the late "Rod Stieger." Ron was present when his sculpture of the "Actor" was presented to "Rod Stieger." The following year Ron's sculpture of the "Actor" was given to several Hollywood celebrities. Ron was also hired by the "Medallic Art Company" to help with the sculpture and production of medals such as the famed "Peabody." Ron helped in the striking of the medals that were awarded to the late Lady Bird Johnson, Maria Shriver, Jon Stewart and of the Bob Hope Award which was presented by then President Clinton to John Glenn for his being selected by NASA to ride in the Space Shuttle at age 77. In 2003 the Governor of Montana, Judy Martz, presented President George Bush with one of Ron's wood carvings. So to say the least Ron has earned his reputation in the art world as one of the best in his field of sculpture.

Whitebull

Lift Off

Falcon

Standing on a Corner

West Blue Birds

Stone Chief

Aletha Deuel

The dusty hues of the cacti, the rusty red of the rocks and the purple mountain shadows lend themselves well to this Arizona born Artist. Aletha remembers moving to her grandparents homesteaded wheat section in the Northwest part of the Kansas plains, where she also felt at home. Moving to Washington State in the late 50's, she paints the grandeur of the Northwest with passion and love. With her mother living in Phoenix, she returns as often as possible to the place that is dearest to her heart, the Southwest. A trip to Nairobi, Kenya, and The Great Rift Valley Africa in 1998, a trip to Guatemala in 2000 and Fiji in 2001 and 2004 gave her many new painting subjects and experiences.

Aletha's work is shown throughout the Northwest and is in numerous corporate art collections. Most recent honors include the Washington State's Historical Museum's Tall Ship Show. Other shows and Galleries include: The Street of Dreams, The Western Washington Fair Art Show, Handford Art Gallery, The Metropolitan Park Department, Seahurst Gallery in Burien, Washington and Gallery 1 in Ellensburg, Washington. Aletha also participates in the National Show, Celebration Western Art (Oldfield Production Company), The Western Washington Fair Grounds, Puyallup, Washington. Local shows and awards are too numerous to list.

Aletha loves to paint on location as much as possible and believes her talents are a gift from God and the patience of the many wonderful instructors she has had the privilege to study with. Instructing at Colleges, and Art Centers with all ages, she remains a student of Art herself, for Life.

Aletha has donated many paintings to different scholarships for Aspiring art students and other charities. She donates her time to local schools on career day, and is also available for Lectures and Art Demos in art clubs and other groups.

Aletha Deuel

5001 144th St East
Tacoma, Washington 98446

1-253-537-6058

Margie Jackson

www.mjacksonstudios.com

Growing up in Oklahoma, not far from the Fort Sill Reservation, Margie spent her early years in an isolated atmosphere, her horse and her dog as her only companion. In the evenings the haunting sounds of the Indian drums could he heard. Days were spent riding, helping to herd cattle and listening to the stories of the old cowboys who were her friends. Needing an outlet for her creative drive, Margie would draw with any material at hand, sculpting figures from soap or clay from the creekbed.

Since those early years, Jackson has become an internationally recognized artist, with work in corporate, private and municipal collections both here and abroad. She has illustrated magazines and corporate publications. She has illustrated, written and designed the public relations book for a municipal chamber of commerce and also collaborated on the logo for the city of Yelm, Washington. Margie has won numerous awards and has been included in prestigious invitational and juried shows nationwide. Her work has been represented in several magazines and publications, including Artwest, Southwest Art, Western Horseman, Art n Arizona, Bechtel Magazine and many more.

Although Margie created many of her early works with no formal art training, she has since studied at Western Wyoming College, University of Hartford, The House of Bronze, as well as many other workshops with other well known artists, including Edward Fraughton-Master Sculptor. Margie has also actively shared her knowledge with others through presenting her own workshops.

Margie, her husband Billy and their four small children traveled extensively for many years, finally settling on a small farm outside Yelm, Washington. Margie spent her days in the peaceful atmosphere of her studio overlooking LaCamas Creek. Around her were gathered her horses, cattle and many other assorted animals. There, she was able to create in bronze and to paint her impressions of life, achieving a beauty only possible through intimate knowledge of her subject matter. Jackson is equally proficient in portraying the human form in any setting. Animals and humans seems to come alive in her skilled hands.

Margie and her husband Billy now maintain a home and studio in the Historical district of the City of Lacey, Washington, along with a small gallery showroom where she continues to paint and sculpt.

Moon of the Greasy Grass

Into the Shining Mountains

Daddy's Girl

Ancient Ways

If you are interested in contacting Margie Jackson please email her at mjack91417@aol.com

Spring Winds

Geronimo Clark

405 N. 10th Place • Aumsville, OR 97325
Phone (503)749-2474• E-mail g_m_clark@yahoo.com
www.angelfire.com/hi3/geronimoworld

Heart Within

Winter Magic

Your Not Alone

Tiny Tigers

Since appearing in the last edition of The Northwest Artists coffee table book, Geronimo's career has taken several different turns. He tried his hand at running his own art gallery, he did several commissions of historical buildings for the Stayton Historical Society, he once again served as the commemorative artist for the Oregon Covered Bridge Festival, he designed a exclusive original for the Daughters of the American Revolution and also did a proto-type design for a War Memorial that the Stayton Oregon DAR Chapter wanted to build. In 2007 Geronimo made new friends by donating a large original to the Salem Friends of the Feline, a charity that provides rescue for homeless felines.

Geronimo has been working on new techniques of sculpting hide, trying some different types of images, but finds himself always returning to the Neo-Native American art he does so well. His art will be available at the new Spirit Mountain Casino art gallery in mid 2008.

Geronimo currently resides in Aumsville, Oregon with his wife of 20 years, two teenage daughters, and nine cats.

Cody (buffalo) appeared in movie "Dances with Wolves"

Ken The Buffalo Man

Kenneth J. Hurley

Renowned Western Wildlife Artist

360.942.3808 • 31 Smith Creek Road, Raymond, WA 98577

Kenneth J. Hurley, known in Western circles as the Buffalo Man, is a self-taught artist...although his subject matter reflects history and wildlife, the buffalo is his specialty and artistic first love. Among many awards he received is "The Producer's Award" at the 36th Annual Spokane Western and Wildlife Art Show held February 24-26, 2006 at Spokane, Washington. He also created the art work for the cover of "Rockin' HW" cd title "A Night 'Round the Wagon" plus the artwork on the back cover and on the cd itself in 2007. Hurley's paintings and sketches have been exhibited in all major shows in the Northwest where he has won a myriad of honors and awards. He has participated in many one and two man shows, including one in Panama. He is also very well known for his Quick Draws at the shows. Kenneth has traveled extensively in Africa, Costa Rica, Panama, Honduras, Jamaica, England, and other countries. Sketching and photographing the wildlife and landscape of the countries. Kenneth also has participated in major shows in Montana for the past twenty years and is well recognized there. In addition to painting, Hurley has been the Washington State Competitive Trail Ride Champion seven times and the rider of the year on eight occasions. Also available are remarques, originals, limited edition prints, postcards, notecards, cribbage boards and t-shirts. He also does commissions. He works in watercolor, oil, pencil, pen and ink. Kenneth is a member of Art Ride in South Dakota, Western Heritage Artists in Great Falls, Montana, The Western Art Association in Ellensburg, Washington and the Fred Oldfield Western Heritage Center in Puyallup, Washington.

*Great Spirit

*New Life

*Medicine Wheel - East Guard

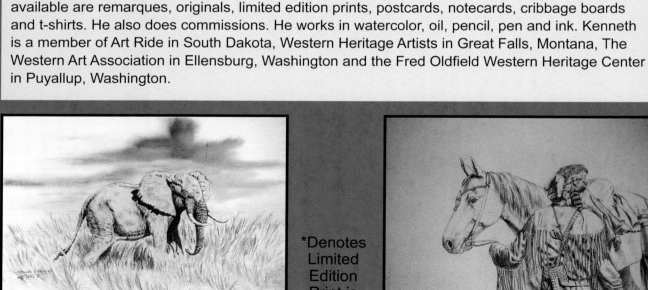

Elephant

Break Time

*Denotes Limited Edition Print is Available

*Rodeo Dog

*Water Break

*Old Broken Horn

*Let's Rodeo

*Warrior Pride

*First Snow

*Past - Present - Future

*His Land

Dreams of Yesterday

*Mt. Rainier Elk

*His First Robe

ART SHOWS PROUDLY PRESENTS THE 2006

PRODUCER'S AWARD
TO
KENNETH J. HURLEY

THIS AWARD IS PRESENTED FOR HIS TALENT AND DEVOTION TO THE WORLD OF FINE ART. HE IS OFTEN REFERRED TO AS THE TRUE PERSONIFICATION OF A REAL WESTERN ARTIST. HIS HONESTY IS ABOVE REPROACH; HIS CHARACTER BEFITS THE TRUE AMERICAN COWBOY. HIS DEVOTION TO THOSE AROUND HIM IS BEYOND REPROACH. HE HAS LONG BEEN IDENTIFIED AS THE FINEST BUFFALO PAINTER IN AMERICA. WE APPRECIATE HIS SAGE ADVICE AND WE CONSIDER HIM A FRIEND AND A PRODUCER'S ARTIST.

SPOKANE WESTERN & WILDLIFE ART SHOW

Don and Gert Walsdorf with Kenneth J. Hurley

Bill Carnahan

Bill has been painting in oils for over 40 years and teaching basic painting for nearly 40 years. He has shown in many of the larger western art shows as well as smaller arts and craft shows in Washington and Oregon. He enjoys painting wildlife, old barns and flowers of the Pacific Northwest. Now he is focusing more on the teaching. Bill has enjoyed teaching from the beginning, but after being certified with the Bob Ross Company 15 years ago it has become even more enjoyable. He teaches landscapes, seascapes and flowers in his classes. Bill has been traveling across the state teaching hundreds of students over the past 15 years. "It is exciting to help someone that has never painted before to become successful. You do not have to have any experience to take classes and be successful." He will travel anywhere in the State of Washington for a group of 6 or more people interested in learning the Joy of Painting at a very reasonable fee. If you are interested or to get more information, contact Bill via email at wood-n-acres@juno.com or call him at 509-966-7588. You will be glad you did.

▲ White Delight

▲ Morning Mist

Watchful Eyes ▶

Afternoon Rest ▲

Idaho Barn ▲

Spot ▲

Days Gone By ▲

Wildlife and scenic art
of the Pacific Northwest

PO Box 8083 • Yakima, Washington 98908
(509) 966-7588

◄ **Up To The Top**

Neon Rainbow ►

Julie Thompson

Spanaway, Washington • 253.875.5055
www.featherlady.net • Email: featherlady@comcast.net

Pacific Northwest artist Julie Thompson has been creating her intricate paintings on naturally-molted peacock feathers since 1990. Her first markets were along the cruise ship route in the southeast of Alaska, her home state - in such towns as Ketchikan and Skagway. Since then her style has grown and representation has spread to many galleries, in several states, on both coasts. These unique works of art have found homes in collections across the US and Canada as well as in Germany, Ireland, and Japan.

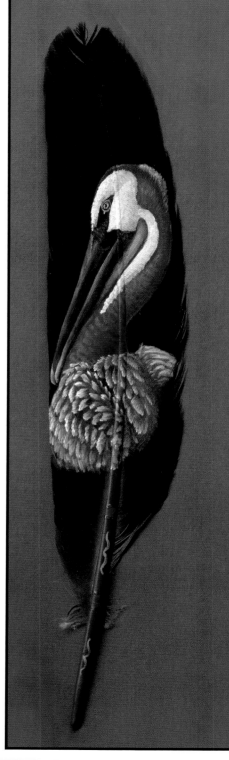

Jody Menge

Libby's Downstream Photo

CMR Elk, Ursa River

Defiance

Jody Menge was born a fourth-generation Montanan, raised on a ranch; which ingrained a love of nature and of the spectacular grandeur in the western landscape.

Now an award-winning painter; she holds a bachelor of fine arts degree, shows in many prestigious western galleries and museums; she also had a recent solo show at the Montana State Capitol. Jody has work in collections all over the United States, and in several foreign countries. She's a member of Western Heritage Artists, and has been a featured artist for Pheasants Forever, Walleyes Unlimited, and other organizations and participates in important art auctions yearly.

Jody currently works in gouache and acrylic, recently focusing on the landscapes of the Missouri River Breaks in Central Montana, she also has an interest in painting ethereal nightscapes, and wildlife.

"I have a deep attachment to Montana and it's breath-taking beauty, both harsh and serene; there is endless inspiration for me here; in the abundant wildlife, the expansive vistas, the intense colors, the uniqueness of light. I try to capture the essence of these places in my work."

Website: www.jodymenge.com
Email: jmenge@midrivers.com

R. Diane Martinez

715 Braught Road Bosque Farms, New Mexico 87068 • email: cmail450@aol.com • 505.869.6035

R. Diane Martinez to say the least is a very talented potter. Thirty years ago she developed a unique style of contemporary blackware. Each piece is handmade and free hand designed. She includes intricate designs on the inside and out of all her pieces. Ms. Martinez has won many awards for her pottery. She has won the New Mexico State Fair's pottery award for 28 years in a row. Over the years she has won more than 575 first place ribbons, trophies, and major awards. Ms. Martinez has also been recognized in newspapers, magazines, books, and films. She was recognized as one of the "2000 Notable American Women." Ms. Martinez has traveled across the U.S. showing her work at major art markets. She has been featured artist for many of them.

Besides her pottery Ms. Martinez is a very busy woman. She has a husband, five children and a miniature zoo at her house. Ms. Martinez has done everything from Scouts to coaching girls soccer. Ms. Martinez was raised in Gallup, NM. The beauty that surrounded her as a child inspired her to pursue a career in art. The beautiful red rocks and the nearby forests were her playground.

Ms. Martinez says her artistic goal is "to take a piece of New Mexico's earth and shape it, decorate it, so the finished pot reflects the rich beauty that surrounds me at my home. When people take a piece of my pottery home I want them to remember the magic and the spirit of New Mexico. Each pot is a piece of my heart that goes home with people around the world." Her award winning art work can be purchased on the Santa Fe Plaza in good weather or by appointment from her studio in Bosque Farms, NM. Ms. Martinez has collectors of her pieces worldwide.

The Spell of the Flute

**Chief Joseph
Limited Edition Bronze**

cameron blagg

Ron Boyd

"I'm told my eccentricity as well as my egocentricity are rivaled only by my creativity," Ron explains.

Attending Portland State College in the 1960's, Ron majored in architecture, while dabbling with various art forms from start to finish. Taking a break from his studies, he began a temporary career as a portrait photographer that lasted over 30 years. This was a period of exploration for Ron as he tampered with woodcarving, printmaking, stained glass, ink drawing and jewelry.

Ron began painting with a passion after his health went south, preventing him from keeping even a part time job. It was late September 2000 when he started work on "The Red Lady." Ron says that he "sort of punked around at it and others for a couple of years." As his artwork began to pile up, space became an issue. His solution: Show and Market.

Stylistically, his art is varied from classic to surreal, impressionist to neo-modern and to quote Ron, "The much sought after Ronism." His subject matter includes inventive fantasies, forestscapes and flowers, fish and birds, river scenes, still lifes, historical pieces and portraits and more.

He is bold and not afraid to just do something and feed on it. He likes to take a series of photographs when doing represental artworks because it helps him understand the subject and its surroundings more deeply. The finished painting tends to invoke an emotional and nostalgic feeling in the viewer. When an imaginary subject is the project at hand, the vision develops and reveals itself during the process - "Starting also helps," says Ron. "I begin with a line or two, letting the line take me where it will and I follow it. Like being lost in the woods, the goal will reveal itself."

Ron's advice to artists just starting out: "Don't waste time worrying about how good you are. Just get off the couch and paint. Put paint on the canvas. Move the brush. A little each day and good will come. Eat, breathe and sleep art. That's all!"

Ron's paintings and prints are available at
The Gilbert District Gallery in Seaside, Oregon
Contact Ron Directly at 503.739.0364

cameron blagg

Southwest Art

Story Time

Ghostdancer Bronze

In thirty years of oil painting, Blagg has developed his own unique style, his talent driven by the desire to make painting his life's work. Blagg has been painting professionally since 1974. As a self-taught artist, he has a reputation for his originality, imagination and authenticity. "His reading is of history, his collecting of the past...It is the past which fascinates him, the past which he paints." - Ray Summers, KOIN-TV, Portland, Oregon

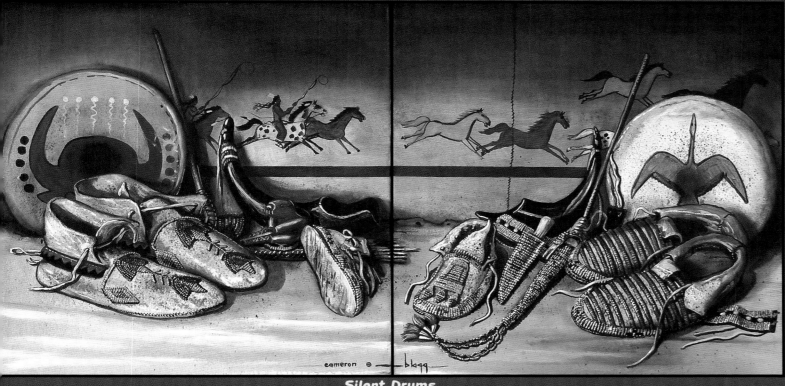

Silent Drums

Hold it Right There

Navajo Saddle

Kiowa Cradleboards

The Fred Oldfield Western Heritage Center

85 years of Washington state history seen through the life of artist,
Fred Oldfield

Our 5400 sq. ft. facility, conveniently located just inside the Red Gate at the Puyallup Fairgrounds, houses authentic artifacts within old west dioramas, an extensive gallery of Fred Oldfield original artwork, a magnificent native american basket collection, and a gift shop of FOWHC memorabilia and artwork by local artists. It is the home for many ongoing art classes for the youth, as well as specialty classes for adults. The FOWHC is also a great place to hold special events with an old west feel.

Come on down and join us for some down home hospitality and history!
Please call for a tour, or visit our website for open hours, special events, and more information.

866-445-9175 • www.fredoldfieldcenter.org

Michael

Oregon Scenes
Izzy Fletcher
Pleasant Hill, Oregon

Growing up in the foothills of the Oregon Cascades, Izzy paints the beauty of places and creatures we all see and enjoy. "Loving the outdoors her family has spent many weekends camping, fishing and exploring. Trips across the mountain passes with streams and rivers rushing down to the valley on the way to the Pacific Ocean and the habitat as we travel on. This I love putting to my canvas in acrylic, watercolor and oil".

Website: www.emeraldartcenter.org
Email: izzy_fle@epud.net • 541.747.2661

Port of Ilwaco
SATURDAY MARKET

May thru September

Artist Inquiries Call:
Sharon 360-244-1514

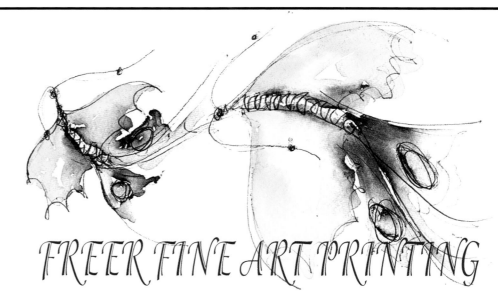

FREER FINE ART PRINTING

SPECIALTY GICLEE PRINTING FOR ARTISTS by ROSALIND FREER
MAILING ADDRESS: FREER STUDIO - 90336 HWY 101 - WARRENTON - OREGON - 97146
tel. 503-861-9689 e-mail freerprints@harborside.com

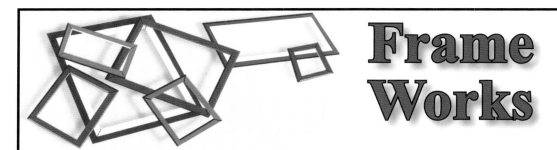

"Good art tells a story,
great art allows the viewer
to participate and finish the story."

-Dave Bartholet-

The Western Heritage Art Show
Over 60 Artists Every Year

Held in the Holiday Inn every March in Great Falls, Montana
Three Floors of Notable Artists

Please visit www.westernheritageartshow.com for more information